Twayne's United States Authors Series

Sylvia E. Bowman, *Editor*

INDIANA UNIVERSITY

Edward Everett Hale

TUSAS 284

Edward Everett Hale

EDWARD EVERETT HALE

By JOHN R. ADAMS
San Diego State University

TWAYNE PUBLISHERS
A DIVISION OF G. K. HALL & CO., BOSTON

Library of Congress Cataloging in Publication Data

Adams, John R   1900–
  Edward Everett Hale.

  (Twayne's United States authors series ; TUSAS 284)
  Bibliography: p. 137 - 40.
  Includes index.
  1. Hale, Edward Everett, 1822–1909—Criticism and
interpretation.
  PS1773.A6   818'.4'09   77-1483
  ISBN 0-8057-7186-7

FOR JANE

Contents

About the Author

Dr. John R. Adams, an experienced writer on literary subjects, is the author of *Harriet Beecher Stowe* of Twayne's United States Authors Series. He received his degrees from the University of Michigan and the University of Southern California where his major interests were literary criticism, the history of philosophy, and American literature. He has taught and lived in Michigan, Washington, and California. At San Diego State University he has been professor and chairman of the English Department, Chairman of the Division of the Humanities, and is currently University Archivist.

Dr. Adams has written on such diverse subjects as Henry James, the teaching of literature, and the regional literature of southwestern California. He has also worked as newspaper correspondent and book review editor. He is a member of Phi Beta Kappa and Phi Kappa Phi, honor societies, and of professional organizations including the American Studies Association, the Modern Language Association, and the Philological Association of the Pacific Coast. His biography appears in *Who's Who in America*.

Preface

The two previous books about Edward Everett Hale (1822–1909) are biographies in which interpretations of his writings are subordinated to accounts of his many diverse activities. The present study reverses that emphasis by discussing his literary productions within the framework of his cultural environment. Born in Boston, a member of a distinguished business and political family, Hale absorbed New England culture at the Boston Latin School and at Harvard College, and developed an early familiarity with the worlds of commercial journalism, trade, and politics. As an ordained minister, he moved without envy or inferiority among his greater literary friends—Henry Wadsworth Longfellow, James Russell Lowell, William Dean Howells—and associated without self-consciousness with senators and presidents from Daniel Webster to Theodore Roosevelt, respectively. With the gradual expansion of his perspective from regional to national scope he became in his old age, as Roosevelt said in 1908, a revered spokesman for liberalism of whom all Americans were proud.

Although Hale as a writer is generally recalled only as the patriotic author of *The Man Without a Country* (1863), he wrote voluminously about many subjects and in many genres. His short stories, rich in unforced humor, include a *sputnik* ("The Brick Moon," 1869) and other mechanical and scientific fancies, along with equally ingenious speculations about the responsibilities of citizenship and the right to personal privacy. His novels involve such themes as the westward movement of the frontier in the early nineteenth century and the preservation of popular democracy in the later era of industrial expansion. His observation of urban problems was notably shrewd, for he diagnosed the needs of society as accurately as the public-spirited elected officials of the period—Hazen Pingree in Detroit, Tom L. Johnson in Cleveland, and others as clear-headed as they. Though the more militant forces of the laborers' associations have long since pushed the elitist reformers into the background, Hale's suggestions for amelioration have not lost pertinency.

My present survey of Hale's writings is more a reminder of what he meant than a reinterpretation. It is intended to stimulate the reader's sympathetic curiosity about such intelligent liberalism as his was in a social era vastly different from our own. Because of the limited recent scholarship about Hale, my material has been restricted (possibly fortunately) to his own writings, published and unpublished, and to the testimony of his contemporaries. Greatly as I admire Hale, I cannot agree with the enraptured newspaper book reviewer who declared, "The public have but one fault to find with him: he does not write often enough." Over five hundred magazine articles, one hundred separate books and pamphlets, are considerably more than enough to classify and describe in an expository survey.

The arrangement of my study is topical, for both the chapters and sections are devoted to the literary types that Hale favored. The first two chapters describe his writings about himself and his friends. The next six discuss his fiction, in both shorter and longer forms; his volumes of history; his writings on ethics and religion. The last chapter includes an account of his reputation and an appraisal of his contribution to American literary culture.

During ten years of systematic work on this project, I have inevitably received help from many more people than I can mention here. I have thanked most of them informally, I hope, but I must acknowledge special appreciation to two fellow workers at San Diego State University whose assistance went far beyond professional obligation: Mrs. Mildred H. LeCompte, now retired, formerly in charge of interlibrary loan services for the San Diego campus library, and Dr. William A. Perkins, professor of English. I greatly appreciate the patience of Dr. Sylvia E. Bowman and her efficient staff for their efforts to enrich the substance and to clarify the expression of my first drafts. My indebtedness to my wife, to whom the book is dedicated, is inexpressible in words.

JOHN R. ADAMS

San Diego State University

Chronology

1865   Participated actively in the first national conference of liberal Protestant churchmen; work resulted in the founding of the Unitarian Church of America; assumed leadership of the second national conference in 1866.

1866   Became a member of the Harvard Board of Overseers and a trustee of Antioch College in Ohio; under the term "the new civilization" extended his ameliorative and reform interests to speaking and writing for a national audience.

1870   Established a monthly cultural magazine, *Old and New*, absorbed by *Scribner's Monthly* in 1875; meanwhile, wrote extensively for *Old and New*, including an influential moral tale of social regeneration, *Ten Times One Is Ten* (1871), and *In His Name* (1873), a popular historical novelette.

1879   Received honorary degree of Doctor of Sacred Theology from Harvard; later honors, Doctors of Laws from Dartmouth in 1901 and from Williams in 1904.

1887   *Franklin in France*, his most substantial history, in collaboration with his son, Edward E. Hale, Jr.

1898   *Works of Edward Everett Hale*, "Library Edition" in 10 volumes (1898–1900), with prefaces and notes by the author.

1900   December 31, midnight, presided at Boston civic ceremony greeting the new century; April 3, 1902, an elaborate public program celebrating his eightieth birthday.

1902   *Memories of a Hundred Years*, an historical and autobiographical record.

1903   Unanimously chosen chaplain of the United States Senate, a position he filled until April 1909.

1909   Attended inauguration of William Howard Taft as president, March 4; illness forced Hale to leave Washington, April 22; last entry in his journal, June 8; death, at Boston, June 10.

1913   May 22, memorial statue unveiled on Boston Common.

1917   Publication of correspondence and diaries in *The Life and Letters of Edward Everett Hale*, by Edward E. Hale, Jr.

CHAPTER 1

Biography and Autobiography

I Biography

FEW men of comparable accomplishment have lived as undramatic, tension-free a life as Edward Everett Hale. From birth to death he enjoyed eighty-seven years of physical vitality, calm nerves, and intellectual vigor. The initial encouragement of Hale's family and friends was broadened by easy stages into city and statewide prominence and led to national acclaim and admiration. Neither external obstacles nor the frustrations of indecision undermined his self-confidence or prevented him from knowing what he wanted to do or from doing it well. As versatile as he was energetic, he could speak, write, persuade, organize, and administer; and he could do each separately or all in unison without consciously sacrificing one talent to another.

The family into which he was born in 1822, as the fourth child, was one of solid Boston respectability that had resided in Massachusetts since the seventeenth century.[1] His grandfather Enoch had been a minister; and his father Nathan, a graduate of Williams College, was a prosperous businessman. He was the owner and editor of the leading Boston newspaper, the *Daily Advertiser*, and also the promoter and president of the Boston and Worcester Railroad. He was the nephew and the namesake of Nathan Hale, the hero of the Revolutionary War whose last words were known to every American as the epitome of patriotism: "I only regret that I have but one life to lose for my country."

The family of Edward Everett Hale's mother was equally distinguished throughout New England, for she was the sister of the versatile Edward Everett (1794–1865) who was famous during his lifetime—though his versatility has by now been forgotten—as an orator, minister, professor of Classics, and magazine editor. Later,

1

he was a congressman from Massachusetts for a decade, a governor of the commonwealth, an ambassador, the president of Harvard, the secretary of state, and a United States senator from Massachusetts. His sister, Mrs. Nathan Hale, was as well endowed and as talented, in her limited sphere, as her famous brother.

Throughout early life, Edward Everett Hale was surrounded by parental love and intelligence. Because the whole family was extraordinarily congenial, he learned more at home through planned activities shared with the older children than from school. His formal education came through the standard sequence of private elementary "dame" school, Boston Latin School, and Harvard College, to each of which he submitted; he was often bored but seldom rebellious. Upon graduation from college at the age of seventeen, with his Phi Beta Kappa key, recognition as class poet, and the second highest scholastic average in the class of 1839, he abruptly terminated his formal education. Dissatisfied with the dull routine of scheduled instruction, he convinced himself that private study for the ministry was better preparation than enrollment in the Harvard Divinity School. His doctor's degrees were honorary and from much later dates: he received a Doctor of Sacred Theology degree from Harvard in 1879, a Doctor of Laws from Dartmouth in 1901 and one from Williams in 1904.

As such recognition indicates, Hale's youthful trust in himself was well founded. He diligently studied religion and many other subjects. He tried teaching, working for two years as Latin teacher in the Boston Latin School, but he much preferred assisting his father and his brothers Charles and Nathan with the family newspaper and with railroad projects. He spoke in public as often as he was asked and was licensed to preach before his twenty-first birthday. After experience as a supply preacher—one for single Sundays or for months at a time, as in Washington, D.C., during the winter of 1844—he felt himself ready for ordination as a minister and accepted a call to the Congregationalist Church of the Unity in Worcester, Massachusetts.

These "Wanderjahre," as he later referred to them, were years of exploration and of planned preparation, not of vacillation or of doubt of his vocation. He already believed that, as his was not to be a cloistered ministry, all constructive activities contributed to his future Christian service. His observation of businessmen and politicians would teach him more about men's needs, he felt, than a seminary course in historical theology. His most valuable experience was, the future revealed, his constant practice in writing. This preoccupation had started in childhood for family entertainment and had continued for publication before his graduation from college when he served as legislative reporter for his father's *Daily Advertiser*.

This initiation as a journalist was soon followed by contributions to magazines as responsible as the *North American Review*. The writing of books and pamphlets was not far in the future, a swelling stream that eventually produced more than two hundred publications, including about seventy books, thirty edited works, and well over one hundred printed addresses, sermons, and other pamphlets. With these and his magazine stories and his innumerable journalistic articles for both church and literary magazines, Hale eventually became noted as a minister who wrote well.

He was also a minister who preached well—for he had an excellent voice and absolute self-possession in the pulpit or on the platform—and a preacher who participated in public affairs. During his ten years at Worcester he had joined, encouraged, or organized a dozen local societies for good works, a trifling number in comparison with those in Boston that later shared his interests or benefited from his prestige. Hale, who remained a minister to the end of his life, served the South Congregational Church of Boston for forty-three years before his resignation in 1899; and he was a chaplain of the United States Senate from 1904 to within two months of his death in 1909.

After Hale's marriage in 1852, his home life duplicated the happiness that he had experienced as a child. His wife, Emily Perkins, belonged to a family as solidly Yankee as his own and as distinguished, for she was the granddaughter of Dr. Lyman Beecher and therefore the niece of the magnetic pulpit orator Henry Ward Beecher and also of Mrs. Harriet Beecher Stowe who soon burst into glory as the author of *Uncle Tom's Cabin*. The completely successful Hale marriage was free from conflicts between parents and children. Sunshine was not perpetual, for the inevitable deaths of relatives and friends, young and old, occurred, along with financial stringencies and the failure of cherished enterprises; but the family was remarkable in its unity of purpose and its cooperativeness in execution.

Literary history offers few parallels to the many and varied collaborations of Hale and close members of his family. From first to last he worked for and with his father on the *Advertiser*, with an elder brother on the *Boston Miscellany* (1842), with one of his sisters on fiction as early as 1850 and as late as 1891, with another sister on a series of children's books, and with one of his sons, who became his father's research and editorial assistant while still in his teens. These continuing congenial associations were broken only by death.

In the tumultuous years preceding the Civil War, Hale maintained consistently antislavery views without subscribing to the "activist" positions of the New England Abolitionists who financed John Brown. The Civil War years themselves witnessed Hale's transformation from a successful local preacher into a national figure. "The Man Without a Country," his story published in the *Atlantic Monthly* for December 1863, was promptly accepted throughout the North as a symbol of patriotism almost as thrilling as the dying declaration of Nathan Hale had been in 1776. The war itself directed his energies into such national organizations as the Sanitary Commission and the Freedman's Bureau. Above all, he had reinterpreted his function as a Christian minister; he had lessened his concern for building a self-enclosed congregation and had strengthened his ambition to promote a genuinely enlightened democracy in the whole of America.

In an unusually introspective letter written to his brother Charles in 1865, Hale surprised himself with its revelation of his "interior life" and with his partly formulated program for his future. "What I know is that I am well, successful, and happy," he wrote; he noted that his wife and children were happy; and he admitted that "I am as near out of debt as a man of my temperament is likely to be." Regarding the ministry, he stated his conviction that "the pulpit gives a man the influence which he must use in other walks and spheres than the pulpit alone." In his words, his life had become very happy: he had no enemies, so far as he knew; his congregation approved of him; he was a leader in the Unitarian denomination, "the advance body in Christian civilization"; and he had more outlets in the press than he could supply.[2]

In this optimistic mood, Hale broadened his participation to include national as well as local movements. He actively supported specific projects for rapid transportation, for the removal of tenements, for a system of national parks, and for a world court. He sponsored more general proposals such as temperance, the association of charitable organizations, and profit sharing in industry. Some of his proposals were popular; others were controversial, and not a few of them were utopian; but all were directed hopefully toward a better future. For this combination of causes—"The New Civilization," as he called it—he spoke, wrote, organized, agitated, not fanatically, but with the insistence of a seer and prophet.

"Look up and not down; look forward and not back; look out and not in; lend a hand" were the mottos by which Hale lived and with which he stimulated many individuals and service-oriented groups into activities like those he promoted. Alert to the needs of his time and true to his faith in humanity, he became a revered old man whose physical voice retained its magic and whose written words conformed to his appearance. He was the image of a sage, the kind of person to whom a monument is appropriately erected in his home town.

II *Autobiography:* A New England Boyhood *(1893)*

Although Hale never wrote a formal autobiography (for *Memories of a Hundred Years* is the misleading title of a book only partly autobiographical), he was not reticent in talking about himself. "There are few people who do not like to talk about themselves," he generalized (*Works*, VI, vi).[3] His most extended consecutive fragments of autobiography are five articles written at the request, as was much of his later work, of an editor—specifically Horace Scudder of the *Atlantic Monthly*, in which they were published in 1892 as "A New England Boyhood." A "padded" book version (to use Hale's adjective) was well received in 1893, under the same title. Reissued in Volume Six of Hale's *Works* (1900), *A New England Boyhood* remained continuously in print for many years; and it was reprinted as late as 1964.

A New England Boyhood is a remarkably specific account of a remarkably untroubled childhood. Its ten chapters begin with a description of Boston in the 1820s—a country town with stagecoaches instead of railroads. Nine solid blocks of buildings, or perhaps a few more, were already in existence; but "all the other buildings stood with windows or doors on each of the four sides, and in most instances with trees, or perhaps little lanes between; as all people will live when the Kingdom of Heaven comes"(1). Furniture, dishes, and carpets were "elegant," and "a decanter of wine would invariably have stood on a sideboard in every parlor, so that a glass of wine could readily be offered at any moment to any guest"(4). Open fires and abundant food were the other comforts of a predominantly rural or village life.

Hale's education began at an early age, even for Boston. Like other intelligent children, he never really liked school because he considered most of his teachers much less intelligent than he was. "I cannot tell how we were taught to read, for I cannot remember the time when I could not read as well as I can now"(10). To Hale, the textbooks, such as a Latin version of *Robinson Crusoe*, were ridiculous as well as monotonous. More satisfactory was the summer swimming school conducted by Francis Lieber (later an eminent political scientist), but dancing school was an embarrassment and a bore.

Hale's real education took place at home, through his parents and his brother Nathan, three years his senior, "to whom I owe most of what I am and have been in the world"(29). Instead of toys, the house was filled with such materials as springs, pulleys, planks, chemical and electrical supplies, carpenter's tools, and printing equipment—"almost everything we wanted for purposes of manufacture or invention"(45). F. W. A. Froebel himself could not have specified an environment more inducive to spontaneous activity.

There were of course outdoor games, as well as "tame" indoor games like checkers and chess; but the principal entertainment must have been reading. The charming sixth chapter, "The Books in the Attic," is a tribute to Hale's childhood favorites. Downstairs, the house was full of books, for "most of the books published in America were sent to my father for review in the *Daily Advertiser*"(92). The children were permitted to read whatever they wished, but their favorites were six or seven volumes in the attic: Sir Walter Scott's minor poems; Maria Edgeworth's *Harry and Lucy;* anonymous compilations like *The Boy's Own Book* ("one hesitates before he writes so great a name") and *The Treasury of Knowledge;* Daniel Defoe's *Robinson Crusoe;* and "sometimes there was a stray second volume of *Don Quixote."* Hale talks laughingly and earnestly by turns about these books and others, but he expresses unparalleled admiration for *Robinson Crusoe:* "that Central Book in Modern Literature, the book which explains all other books to those who cannot understand them without; the book which should have for itself a separate table, shelf, or case"(96).

Admission to Harvard at the age of thirteen years and five months

was, says Hale, "not unusual in those days"; but he, the youngest
freshman of the year, was one of the six applicants among eighty
who passed the qualifying tests without conditions. Never a friend of
examinations, which he labeled at various times as *abominable,
absurd,* and *humbug,* he found the Harvard examinations in Latin,
Greek, and mathematics childishly simple. He considered most of
the classes insipid, but he felt differently about those of Edward T.
Channing in English composition or those of Benjamin Peirce—
father of the pragmatist philosopher C. S. Peirce—in mathematics.
When his classes palled, he resorted to the college library or to the
more exciting new books. Hale was already addicted to current
novels of Edward Bulwer, G. P. R. James, Frances Trollope, and
Mrs. Catherine Gore, as well as to "plenty more, of which names
and authors are now forgotten." In addition, he liked the older
fiction of Scott and Jane Austen, as well as the later stories of Feni-
more Cooper "I doubt if I averaged more than four volumes [two
books] a week. But I am sure I read as many as that, and I think they
did me much more good than hurt"(181).

Hale found formal demonstrations of student academic achievement less thrilling than the Harvard College administration intended them to be. Some Phi Beta Kappa dinners were worth attending, especially the one at which Daniel Webster and Edward
Everett spoke and at which Oliver Wendell Holmes read his own
verses. Class days, as they were called, were deplorable occasions
for drunkenness; and commencements were dreary marathons of six
hours with as many as thirty addresses.

Hale welcomed his graduation as a release from confinement;
later, both as an alumnus and as a member of the Board of Overseers, he softened his criticism by admitting that only two out of
three lectures and recitations had been useless. "If we did not profit
much from the functions of the staff, we had a good deal of time left
to us in which to work out our own salvation"(346). He left Harvard
with the second highest scholastic average in the class of 1839 and
with the additional distinction of his selection as a not very distinguished class poet.

Important as education was to the Boston elite, it is not the sole
topic of *A New England Boyhood.* Church was also important, and
so were food—especially at the Thanksgiving feast—the volunteer
fire department, excursions by carriage, and evening lectures to
which "if you were old enough you took a friend of the other

sex"(126). Hale's picture is rosy, despite his occasional references to disturbances such as the racial riot on Broad Street in 1837 in which "the Irish got well beaten, but the firemen appear to have been as much in the wrong as they"(138). He was not blind to social problems and defects, especially as Boston grew and as the old provincial self-assurance weakened; but social problems oppressed him less in boyhood than in later life when, as a Christian minister, he felt responsible for social amelioration. A stranger omission in an old man's account of his youth is the minor attention paid to family or, indeed, to self: A New England Boyhood is the record of what a young person saw and did publicly; it is not a revelation of his psychological aches and private pains. Presumably, he had none that he wished to share with readers of the Atlantic Monthly.

To complete the sixth volume of his Works, Hale gathered eighteen magazine articles written at various times, among which are a number of autobiographical interest. "Boston in the Forties"(239–252) exaggerates the sympathy that he had felt as a young man with the Transcendental movement, for he was never an adherent, although he was sympathetic to the related activities that he calls "Philanthropy." Only Elizabeth Peabody's bookstore at No. 12 West Street aroused his unreserved admiration; for the patrons who might be met there were Bronson Alcott, James Freeman Clarke, Ralph Waldo Emerson, Nathaniel Hawthorne, Horace Mann, George Bancroft, Oliver Wendell Holmes, and others almost as famous. "Who was there that you did not meet who was wide awake and was interested in the future?" he asked. "You stood and talked there—gossiped if you please—with such people; and you carried off the Revue de Deux Mondes of the month before, or you looked between the leaves of [David Friedrich] Strauss's Leben Jesu, or something else which had appeared from Europe"(246).

Information about Hale's personal life during these years is scanty. His opposition to the extension of slavery was unequivocal; but, a man in his forties during the Civil War, he never volunteered as a soldier. Aside from his writing—for The Man Without a Country was not his only contribution to morale—he was a sergeant in the drill corps and an enthusiastic recruiter: "I said that the moment the enlistment from my church stopped, I should go myself; and I should have done so"(292). Late in the war, he was sent as a messenger to the front during the advance on Richmond; and his account of his one night in camp as he told it in "A Church in the

War," is worth repeating. The cannonading was heavy, but Hale did not realize how unusual it was; therefore, unconcerned and un-alarmed, he slept in comfort. "It was thus that it happened to me that I spent my first and last battle in bed"(306). Although the newspapers printed a story that a terrific battle had "mowed down" Union forces and "decimated" the rebels, what had occurred was that "a party of ladies had been entertained on board one of our ships of war" and an officer, "with the gallantry of his profession," had shown them how a gun was fired. This shot started a noisy chain reaction, but "there was never any evidence that a rabbit was scratched," and "no drop of human blood was shed in that battle of giants"(307).

This ironic anecdote is typical of Hale's view in his autobiography, for he regarded bureaucratic waste as a matter of general interest. He asserted that even in childhood "the outlook which I had on life was the outlook of a journalist"(319). If an incident had public significance, he played it up; but the events of his private life, however meaningful to him, were not to be shared with his readers. Indeed, his only mention of an occasion of great importance to him was a single sentence, "In the year 1852, I married"(289).

III *European Travel*

Much as Hale enjoyed travel, he did not succeed in visiting Europe until he was thirty-seven years old. For each of his five journeys abroad, between 1859 and 1892, he claimed reasons beyond the obvious pleasures of vacation relaxation. In England, he studied welfare agencies; in France, church cooperation or, on one occasion, geography for his historical tale *In His Name;* in Spain, national archives. He solicited manuscripts from distinguished contributors for his magazines, supervised the establishment of a young relative in school, cared for a sick daughter, and verified historical references for friends. Everywhere, he observed transportation facilities with the eye of an ex-professional railroad man, and he filled his notebooks with material for sermons and magazine articles about all subjects with which he was concerned. The two books that are primarily accounts of his European experiences, the major parts of his writings on the subject, are a contribution to his autobiography but not an intentional or systematic record of this phase of his development.

The first of these, *Ninety Days' Worth of Europe* (1860), is an informal, unpretentious book which was never reprinted. Instead of florid descriptions of scenic marvels (except for those about Swiss mountains and about the Rhine country), Hale introduced informative and useful explanations about the superb library services of the British Museum (182–87), where he studied documents for his historical research, and about the cooperative organization of the Protestant ministers of Paris (168–74), which he recommended highly as a model for American cities. Hale's third special interest, European religious services, was treated in the *Christian Register* instead of in the book. Because he avoided as much as he could "speculations" about European politics, he makes few statements as flatly assertive as the one about a situation in Ireland: "The British government met its responsibility nobly in that terrible year" of the Irish famine(213).

Hale, who enjoyed his introduction to European civilization, writes admiringly about French administrative "genius," about English common sense, and about Swiss intelligence. Italy baffled him, but that country was unquestionably a "paradise" of fine art. The statement, "If I had no duties and no friends and no country, I would go to Florence to live"(112) is a tribute with reservations. His comments about Rome are less whimsical than earnest, for his initial contact with clericalism disturbed and alarmed him. Rural England delighted him, but not London streets at night, where "you see that awful division of castes which is the curse of life here"(34).

Hale, a fanatical bibliophile, not only loved to read books, to allude to his favorites, or to quote from them, but also to touch them, to handle them, and to honor the people who manufactured them. "My enthusiasm for Greenough's 'Franklin' makes me look with more interest at other statues of printers," he wrote(66). His bookishness reached its peak during his study at the British Museum, with its "princely hospitality," but only second to him was the library at Cambridge, where he read John Milton's manuscript book containing "Lycidas" and "Comus." Like Samuel Taylor Coleridge earlier, Hale found himself "kneeling before the desk where it was kept"; but, unlike Coleridge, he did so "not in homage, but because that was the convenient attitude for reading"(21).

Hale's response to treasures of the representational arts was more complicated. As the friend of Richard Greenough and William Wetmore Story, he was fairly confident of his judgment of sculpture (on the basis also of plaster replicas that he had studied in the Boston Athenaeum); and he made no secret of his enthusiasm for Story, whose Roman studio he visited and described in detail (141–48).

But, since painting was an unfamiliar art to Hale, he began his inspection tour with due modesty: "I have doubted very seriously whether, because I know so little of it all, fine galleries might not overpower me, alarm me, and fail to please me"(27).

Within a week, his worst fears about his capability to judge art had been overcome; for his confidence had rapidly developed: "There is no doubt at all, that, if you brought any bright child of ten years into these galleries, he would select as the best painters those whom the world has selected"(89). After trying the experiment on himself, he admitted that "I did not quite come up to the 'masterly' selection I have claimed one could make"(93). Sober afterthought led to the confession, "I should not dare say that I should select the same forty [artists] on any other day"(93). Even professional critics have not always been so frank as this novice connoisseur.[4]

If *Ninety Days' Worth of Europe* reveals a minister of whom a congregation might be proud, *Seven Spanish Cities* (1883) is a much better book—a more skillful combination of personal narrative, historical background, and chatty advice about how to travel by train and coach.

"Why should this man write a book about Spain, when he was there so short a time?" Hale asks in his preface. "That is a very fair question," he admits; "the answer is chiefly personal." Hale had taught himself to read Spanish when he was a Harvard undergraduate, and he had used the language regularly while working on the *Advertiser*. He mentions that his uncle Alexander Everett had been American Minister Plenipotentiary to Spain in the 1820s, and that Washington Irving had been a member of his staff. Thus Hale's boyhood curiosity, aroused by family letters from Spain, had developed into a permanent interest that had led to his collecting documents and to his ambition, never realized, to write a comprehensive "History of the Pacific Ocean and its Shores." The Madrid archives were his special destination in 1882.

The bulk of Hale's book is straight narrative and description, but the style is informal, one that befitted weekly articles published in the *Boston Commercial Bulletin* of his friend Curtis Guild. The main topics are geography, transportation, worship, museums, and archives. He found transportation much better than the British guidebooks reported, both by rail and by stagecoach; but he enjoyed a coach more, particularly when he shared the driver's seat and on occasion took the reins. The forms of Spanish worship puzzled him: "such worship affects a person not trained to it as it might affect a visitor from the planet Mars"(123). He had no such reservations about either the museums or the archives. His appreciation of Spain was general, except for bullfights (which he avoided); and he liked the people, whom he characterized variously as courteous, efficient, and moral: "Certainly there is hope for a people of whose country even the grumbling English guide-books confess that a woman may travel alone in any part of Spain, and shall not anywhere be in any danger of insult"(324).

Almost equally to the Spaniards' credit is the story that Hale tells about Perro Poco—Francis the dog—a Madrid municipal pet that had been granted the privilege of watching the bullfights. "Alas! poor Poco went once too often"(201). On Sunday, June 18, 1882, he was accidentally slashed by a matador; and, while he hovered for weeks between life and death, he became the talk of the town. His picture was on display everywhere, music was composed in his honor, and "two rival journals were issued wholly in his interest, of which all the contents were devoted to supposed anecdotes of Perro Poco, or other dog news"(198). The story, as Hale tells it, deserves a place in collections of canine lore for dog lovers.

IV   *The March of a Century*

Hale's book that was finally entitled *Memories of a Hundred Years* grew from a series of articles in the *Outlook* between November 1901, and October 1902.[5] It is a fine production for a man of eighty years; and the publisher, Macmillan, provided the handsome format it deserved. Neither autobiography nor history exclusively, it is a personally concocted combination of the two. History is viewed through a keyhole—as Hale repeatedly reminded his readers—and is illustrated by private reminiscences, seasoned with the *obiter dicta* permitted to distinguished men, and marred by the factual mistakes inseparable from old age.

The first half of the book, which describes the nation in 1800, is questionable as either history or autobiography—a clearer title was considered but discarded, "The March of a Hundred Years"—but the second half, in which Hale discusses events he had observed as a mature man, is vivid and atmospheric. On many pages it approaches autobiography, though Hale keeps close to his primary purpose of interpreting broad national movements rather than recalling his private experiences. When he mentions such trivia as the first wheatfield or the first gold coin he ever saw, he does so to illustrate a topic of more than individual significance. His perspective is neither ministerial nor reformist, for he barely mentions his clerical friends or fellow reformers. Instead, he writes as the intellectual journalist that he was and as an alert citizen.

The sources upon which Hale drew transcended those of the ordinary journalist. In addition to his superb memory—which he playfully overpraised as "a memory of iron, which seldom deceives me"(I, 3)—he had his carefully kept diaries, to which he refers sparingly.[6] He also had his father's papers from 1810, his brother Nathan's correspondence with Lowell, and a mass of similar exclusive material. The resulting book still has documentary value as well as readability.

Hale's personality is revealed as a combination of humility with "a certain arrogance" for which he apologized (II, 279), but only in words. His contempt for what he called "the Virginia Dynasty," starting with Thomas Jefferson, was extreme. James Madison's presidency was "tragedy"(I, 186), and James Monroe was a "cipher" who "drifted" into the presidency, mainly because "nobody was afraid of undue abilities in a man who had never shown any ability so far"(220). Fortunately for the country, according to Hale, conspicuous politicians are relatively unimportant. Technological inventions, such as Eli Whitney's cotton gin, and improvements in transportation, such as Robert Fulton's steamship, have been vastly more significant.

Hale's "snapshots," as he calls them, of later nineteenth century America are not random views; they are the record of a notable physical and moral progress. "The physical power at almost every man's hand is now [1901] a thousand times greater than it was in 1801"(II, 223) because of the development of water power and other sources of energy; and knowledge has spread also, for the "enlargement" of life, both individual and national. The Civil War, a calamity in itself, was an advance toward the abolition of slavery; but complete freedom for the ex-slaves was "a business . . . which is not finished yet"(98).

The reception of *Memories of a Hundred Years* was so favorable, both as magazine articles and as a book, that a sequel was arranged immediately. Under the title *Tarry at Home Travels*, a series of articles began in the *Outlook* in the issue of May 5, 1905; and these articles were published in October 1906, by Macmillan in a generously illustrated volume. The subject of travel within the United States was a favorite with Hale, who had tramped through New England in youth and whose fondness for stagecoaching had been succeeded by an equal zest for travel by rail. The reminiscences casually scattered through the book became Hale's last contributions to his autobiography.

Personal though the book is, by intention as well as in fact, it is not primarily a personal history. As the title page states, "My mind impels me to write on places where I have been and of some of the people whom I have seen in them." An entire introductory chapter is an amplification of that statement. "I will try here," he writes, "mostly by memories, sometimes by expectations, with an occasional word of the present fact, to interest the average reader in some plan for seeing some part of his own home, which he has never seen until now"(9–10). Hale followed this announced program consistently except that his travels for these articles never spread beyond New England, New York, and the District of Columbia. His lively reports on New England, his only true home, are expressed with sympathy and understanding. His description of New York is perfunctory, but he does extremely well for Washington, D.C., in two chapters that are not properly part of his vacation tarryings: "Washington Then and Now" and "The New Washington."

The autobiographical contents of these papers are mostly abridged versions of Hale's earlier writings. They include genealogical data(26, 124, 245); a description of his birthplace(145); a tribute to his father(22); college reminiscences(30); references to his work in New Hampshire as a junior geologist(28); allusions to his residence in Worcester(183) and his summer home in Rhode Island(208). Though none of this material is new, it is zestfully presented, as are his longer tributes to Samuel Longfellow, the poet(55); to Henry Longfellow, the professor(59); and his passing compliments to William Dean Howells(3), Sarah Orne Jewett(74), and Rudyard Kipling(135).

In comparison, Hale's anecdotes about celebrities whom he knew are usually disappointing. That Asa Gray appreciated botanical specimens is not surprising, nor that John Ruskin appreciated portfolios of drawings, nor that James G. Blaine—whose friends had given him the sobriquet of "the magnetic statesman"—spoke eloquently, nor that General U. S. Grant enjoyed hearing an account of an ancestor's bravery, nor that George Bancroft used copies of British documents. More indicative of Hale's talents is the account of how easily he thwarted the Anglo-American bureaucracy and obtained desired manuscripts directly from the keeper of the records (who happened to be Sir Francis Palgrave, the anthologist of the famous *Golden Treasury*) before the official request had started its long journey from clerk to clerk.

Other glimpses reveal Hale in less expected moments, when he is selecting the principal of an industrial school, visiting the gallery of the House of Commons, attending Yale's second centennial, praising Theodore Roosevelt as early as 1888, and motoring in a 1906 horseless carriage: "Your chauffeur takes you along the Connecticut Valley at a rate not exceeding fifteen miles an hour, as required by the statute, in those last happy moments before the boiler explodes and you and he leave the study of terrestrial geology"(19).

In one way or another Hale managed to introduce his favorite subjects and to refer to his previous writings. Sometimes he digresses, as in his whimsical demonstration that William Shakespeare's *The Tempest*, in spite of the claims of Bermuda and the West Indies, is based on Captain Bartholomew Gosnold's colonization attempt at Cuttyhunk Island in 1602, so that "Miranda, God bless her! is a Massachusetts girl"(142).[7] Such whimsicality is an essential part of his character; for, expressing his spirit at eighty-four, he is still intent on showing his readers how they can live as happily as he has.

CHAPTER 2

Friends and Acquaintances

I *Who They Were*

ONE of the distinctive marks of Hale's writing was his frequent reference to persons he knew. A mannerism that grew with the years, it is especially noticeable in the reminiscences that he wrote after seventy. As a "grand old man," he was expected by his readers to connect the past with the present, a function that he fulfilled with recognized grace. No question of his honesty was raised, for he had undoubtedly visited Dolly Madison in her home and John Quincy Adams in his. Hale was a man active into the twentieth century; he was a friend of Theodore Roosevelt and of William Howard Taft; his personal recollections extended back to Washington Irving; and he had many times listened to the senatorial debates of Daniel Webster (whom he knew well) before the outbreak of the Civil War. In comparison with such glamor, Hale's biased judgments or occasional mistakes in dating were of small consequence to his admirers.

Among Hale's assertions about himself, the statement that he had known every resident of Boston in the early 1840s aroused suspicions that he must have miscalculated. In holding his ground, he reminded his critics that Boston was then far smaller than the city of half a million that it had become by 1900. In 1840, the total population was ninety-three thousand, of whom forty or fifty thousand were "of the lecture-going age" and of whom fewer than twenty thousand were "active men" (*Works*, VI, 244, 239). All of these persons he recognized by sight, he reasserted, if not by name. Though this claim may have been the exaggeration of his old age, it was not the reckless inaccuracy with which he has been charged; in fact, it was more restrained than the claim of his friends that "every child in Boston had sat on his knee, from Beacon Street to the byways and lost alleys."[1] In his later years, at any rate, every Bostonian had the opportunity of knowing him. At midnight on December 31, 1900, he opened the mass meeting on Beacon Hill where all Boston was invited to greet the twentieth century. The ceremonies were never forgotten by the participants, and the image of Hale's reading from the Book of Psalms was one of the most impressive moments.

True enough, in his writings Hale showed no reluctance in referring casually to important friends; but he did so neither as a logroller nor as a publisher of exaggerated praise. Brief allusions and references to persons—as often living as dead; less often, fictional—were data that he used to explain ideas. Magazine articles and sermons about individuals came naturally from his public activities. His long life encouraged the writing of obituary tributes and festival eulogies of established celebrities.

Among persons still remembered by today's readers, Hale wrote about some from his own youth, such as William Ellery Channing, the churchman to whom the Unitarian denomination is forever indebted; and the historian George Bancroft (1800–1891), whose longevity rivaled that of Hale himself. Hale also wrote several articles about John Greenleaf Whittier, the Quaker poet and journalist. James Freeman Clarke was the clerical associate about whom Hale had most to say. He also wrote formal articles about Henry Bellows and Thomas Starr King, but none about William Henry Furness, who was clearly as respected a friend as they. Among relatives outside the immediate family group, Hale wrote freely about his uncles Alexander and Edward Everett—including three articles on the latter—and prepared a Hale family genealogy which was published in 1856.[2] The only younger relative about whom he wrote in detail was his very distant cousin Helen Keller, the deaf-blind girl whose accomplishments amazed the world.

Hale's articles and addresses were not exclusively about celebrities. He wrote with no greater zest about Phillips Brooks, the noted pulpit orator, than about less eminent clergymen like E. W. Donald, George E. Ellis, Rufus Ellis, and Andrew P. Peabody. He wrote equally appreciatively about Charles Sumner, the famous Massachusetts senator, and about Lorenzo Sabine (1803–1877), a less conspicuous politician and businessman, and about Daniel Lothrop, the publisher. Hale's long association with the American

Antiquarian Society led to tributes to Samuel Jennison, its secretary and librarian, and to Stephen Salisbury, its president.[3]

II *Lowell and Other Literary Friends*

Two of Hale's books are large-scale tributes to close friends, James Russell Lowell and James Freeman Clarke. Because of their more widely known subject, Hale's recollections of Lowell received more public attention, although the book lacks most of the solid virtues that have preserved his edition of Clarke's diary and correspondence as the standard authority. Though Hale knew Lowell well for more than fifty years, his book *James Russell Lowell and His Friends* (1899) is neither systematic biography nor patchwork reminiscence. It had its origin in a request from the *Outlook* for a biography, which Hale declined, and in a later suggestion, which he accepted, for "a review, as it were, of the last sixty years among literary and scientific people in Boston and its neighborhood" (i). Hale started work in April 1897; a series of twelve articles began in the *Outlook* in January 1898; and the enlarged version, a handsome volume produced by the Riverside Press, was published by Houghton, Mifflin and Company with Hale's preface that was dated April 1899. By this time, Lowell had been dead for almost eight years; and Hale had celebrated his own seventy-seventh birthday.

With Lowell as the central character, Hale was encouraged to write freely on topics associated with him. "It must be remembered," he stated, "that this book is not so much a history of his life, as an effort to show the circumstances which surrounded his life and which account for the course of it"(101). Many of these circumstances paralleled those of Hale's own life so closely that the book became a kind of oblique autobiography. The several chapters about Harvard describe Hale's Harvard more certainly than Lowell's, and such a chapter as "Lowell's Experience as an Editor" would need few changes to fit Hale's autobiography, if he had chosen to write one.

Hale's book is no longer essential for an evaluation of Lowell's importance. It is uncritical, and it lacks the twentieth century condescension that sometimes dismisses Lowell as a failure. To Hale, Lowell remained the same wonderful fellow whom he first knew as a Harvard student: he was the BMOC—big man on campus—the one genius certain to succeed; and the bosom friend of Nathan Hale, the older brother whom Hale worshiped idolatrously. Lowell's New

England ancestry, hardly less illustrious than Hale's own, and the Lowell family's tradition of religious toleration and political conservatism provided the substantial basis for a congenial friendship unshaken by later divergence of careers and differences of opinion.[4]

Hale's personal comments, loosely connected with Lowell but appropriate in context, are characteristically pointed. Always irritated by dullness, he renewed his indignant protests against educational waste. In contrast to the mechanical assignments and the poor teaching that had plagued him at Harvard, he repeated with approval Barrett Wendell's account of how, under Lowell's inspiration, a student could learn to read Dante in a month(140). Unlike simple or bumptious youthful ignorance, which Hale took for granted, pretentiousness, whether ornate or pseudoprofound, irked him. He never grasped the significance of Henry David Thoreau, for Hale preferred more conventional "men of letters" who mixed readily with their worldly fellows—men like Benjamin Franklin, John Lothrop Motley, Washington Irving, and Lowell himself, who had written for everyone and, equally important, had "given the world about all the good [American] diplomacy which the world has ever had"(213).[5]

Next to Lowell, the literary contemporaries about whom Hale wrote most were Oliver Wendell Holmes and Ralph Waldo Emerson. For Holmes, he had the special attachment of youthful enthusiasm. The older man, an 1829 Harvard graduate, was a familiar campus figure in Hale's undergraduate years; and Hale's first impression was formed at a college dinner meeting in 1836. Later, the two men had much in common—a gift for conversation, an active sense of humor, an unemotional religion, and a veneration for Boston culture inseparable from Boston Brahmins. On this broad basis, their friendship lasted through life. As old men, they exchanged light birthday poems, but Holmes's was somewhat the lighter type. Between 1889 and 1894, the date of Holmes's death, Hale wrote several complimentary but largely repetitious magazine articles about him.

As a boy, Hale was initially hostile to Emerson; and his complete reversal of judgment is a unique act of reparation for youthful arrogance. Indoctrinated by Cambridge propriety and skeptical of Concord eccentricity, young Hale—who had dipped into Emerson's *Nature* without pretending to understand it—listened unimpressed to Emerson's "American Scholar" address of 1837. He left not only unimpressed—presumably one of the few potential Phi Beta Kappans so resistant to Emerson's inspirational oratory—but positively repelled. "It was not very good," he wrote in his journal, "but very transcendental." Hale's recollections of this historic occasion, which differ from those of others in the audience, was that Emerson's listeners responded with surprise, indignation, and covert criticism. "I remember how afterwards men and women freely said he was crazy."

Emerson's divinity school address annoyed Hale even more. "I did not like it at all," he wrote in his journal on July 15, 1938. He found it in "singularly bad taste" as an attack on the distinguished faculty, and he predicted that, since Emerson had exhausted his "stock of startling phrases concerning soul, mind, etc.," his reputation would fall accordingly.[6] Precisely when Hale recovered from such youthful blindness is not clear, but the process was well under way in 1849. By then, as a young minister at Worcester, he was managing or sponsoring a series of Emerson's lectures there. In 1855, Emerson was inviting Hale to be his house guest at Concord.

By the time of Emerson's second Harvard Phi Beta Kappa address in 1867, Hale was one of "the good brave men" with Lowell and Richard Henry Dana, Jr., as Annie Fields called them in her journal, who immediately surrounded the lecturer.[7] In Hale's writing about this 1867 meeting, he contrasted the enthusiasm of its reception with the mixed reactions of 1837. After thirty years, Emerson sounded neither extravagant nor insane to Hale; and, by 1893, Hale had reached his final estimate of Emerson's greatness. An address delivered in that year, though not Hale's last word, is his final judgment: "The religious teacher who has done most for England and America, and is doing most for England and America today."[8]

After Holmes's death, Hale's only companions among survivors of the Brahmin literary elite were Thomas Wentworth Higginson and Julia Ward Howe, each of whom wrote more about Hale than he did about them. Mrs. Howe—as famous for her "Battle Hymn of the Republic" as Hale was for *The Man Without a Country*—observing that "Boston never drops its H's," was increasingly drawn toward him.[9] Higginson was sometimes less completely complimentary, though he had been a lifelong friend of Hale from college undergraduate years. After hearing Higginson's heated address at the Harvard Divinity School graduation ceremony, Hale had told him, possibly with irony, that he was glad to know a person who was going to "electrify the world."[10] Higginson tried to do so, for he was much more a social activist, in the current sense of the word, than Hale. Nevertheless, the two often worked together; during the 1880s, for example, they combatted anti-Catholicism by supporting parochial schools and they promoted the Socialistic ideas of Edward Bellamy's *Looking Backward.*

III *James Freeman Clarke (1810–1888)*

One of Hale's finest literary and scholarly achievements was his editing of the *Autobiography, Diary and Correspondence* of James Freeman Clarke, his friend of many years and a congenial fellow worker. Unlike the brief obituary tributes and the memorial addresses that Hale was frequently called upon to produce, the volume, which was published by Houghton, Mifflin and Company in 1891, is a substantial one that entailed extensive work by Hale in deciphering, selecting, and arranging fragments of autobiography and correspondence, and in writing numerous connecting links and several complete chapters of narrative.

Hale's apologies for incompleteness, unnecessary as they were, show the seriousness with which he fulfilled his editorial assignment. He had too much material, he said, and too small a space, for proper perspective(411). Nevertheless, the completed volume is an able tribute to a man well worth remembering; it not only presents basic information about him but is also a valuable record of the cultural world in which he lived.

In important aspects, the lives of the two men were similar. Like Hale, Clarke descended from an old New England family. Like Hale, he attended the Boston Latin School, as had his father and both his grandfathers, and Harvard College. Like Hale, he had been too well educated at home to approve of the uninspired formal pedagogy of either institution. Later, like Hale, he was elected an overseer of the college; and, as an alumnus, he discovered values there that he had not appreciated as an undergraduate. "What we did not learn in the regular course of study, we learned outside of it. What we did not acquire from books, we taught each other"(42).

Clarke's graduation from Harvard was followed, as was Hale's, by a period of voluntary exile from Boston, not to Worcester, but to Louisville, Kentucky, where Clarke served his apprenticeship as minister and missionary. By the time he returned to Boston, at the age of thirty, he also had had valuable experience in journalism as a magazine editor and as an occasional contributor to such general periodicals as the *North American Review*. From 1841 to his death in 1888, his main employment, except when interrupted by illness, was, like Hale's, the ministry of a Unitarian church—The Church of the Disciples—but he supplemented this career with voluminous writings, lectures, teaching, and public service. Although Hale does not emphasize their personal friendship, the two men worked together as advocates of many causes, both within and outside their denomination; and their correspondence was on a first name, "dear Edward—dear James," basis.

By temperament Clarke was the more introspective man, for "Dearly as I love nature, humanity has a greater charm for me"(8) is the kind of self-conscious statement that Hale never made about himself. While still a young man, Clarke was friendlier to ideological theorizing than Hale, who was more interested in the printed contents of Elizabeth Peabody's bookstore than in Margaret Fuller's "conversations" that he heard there(143). Perhaps for this reason, Clarke was a more important leader within the Unitarian Church than Hale. It is typical of their relationship that, in the church convention of 1865 that was held in New York, Clarke gave the keynote address and Hale was the secretary. Doctrinally, they were not far apart. Early in his Kentucky ministry, Clarke said, "I believed that every church should have for its first object the teaching of positive Christianity." Therefore he determined to preach "practical Christianity" rather than "to defend Unitarian doctrines as opposed to the Orthodoxy of the place and the time"(72).

Clarke kept his word, for he, no less than Hale, discouraged intolerance and "conscientious bigotry"(40); promoted "emancipation from the chains of dogmatic or of sacramental religion"(206); participated in "gatherings of social reformatory and political parties"(251); and avoided "the ungracious task of controversy as to the text of Scripture"(254). Because of Clarke's work with the Emigrant Aid Company, the Sanitary Commission, the board of trustees of the Boston Public Library, and innumerable other uplift agencies, Hale's motto "lend a hand" was as appropriately Clarke's as it was its creator's. Clarke was over sixty when he published his best book, *Ten Great Religions*, and he was still writing industriously in his seventy-eighth and last year. "I never worry," he declared. "My professional duties as a clergyman have been to me a source of great happiness." Like Hale, "I love work, and especially brain work" (394).

IV   *Friends Farther Removed*

True to Hale's plea for mutual aid, his private acts of friendship
went far beyond a word of praise from the lecture platform, a favorable book notice, or a laudatory article. Numerous kindnesses, large
or small, have been made known by grateful individual recipients;
but many more can be traced through Hale's miscellaneous unpublished letters that are now to be found in eighty institutional libraries.[11] Not significant enough to challenge the validity of Hale's
biographies, this correspondence reveals, as neither of them does,
Hale's unlimited good will and dedication to service. His unselfish
helpfulness was so genuine that it explains, though it may not justify, the "do-good" emphasis that frequently appears as overstate-
ment in his fiction. Like his unforced curiosity about every feature
of the world in which he lived, his generosity needed as wide an
acquaintance as he could make and as many durable friendships as
he could earn.

Among correspondents to whom letters of some substance or significance were addressed, a representative group not mentioned in
the biographies includes Professor Herbert B. Adams, a historian;
Russell A. Alger, a Michigan political figure; Simeon E. Baldwin,
president of the American Bar Association; General Henry Beebe
Carrington and General William Conant Church, writers on military subjects and the latter editor of the *Army and Navy Journal;*
Robert Coit, a railroad president; Elliott Coues, Smithsonian or-
nithologist; Daniel C. Gilman, university president; Samuel Foster
Haven, an archaeologist; Amos A. Lawrence, merchant philanthropist; Henry Demarest Lloyd, muckraking publicist; Joseph
George Rosengarten of Philadelphia, a lawyer and writer on military
history; William Dwight Whitney, editor of the original *Century
Dictionary;* and Theodore Dwight Woolsey, president of Yale University, a clergyman, poet, and political scientist.

These letters are of various kinds as well as about various subjects.
Many are largely devoted to Hale's business as a writer and editor;
others are primarily about church affairs or other good works. Some
are social and ask favors, but more are for the purpose of performing
favors. As a minor service, Hale wrote so many gracious letters of
introduction that he must have enjoyed writing them. As Robert
Collyer, a fellow minister, recalled, Hale had given him a letter of
introduction to the secretary of the British and Foreign Unitarian
Association in London with the result that the Britisher "gave me as

warm a welcome as my heart could desire."[12] The curious special feature is that Collyer, British born, was less well known in England than the American Hale.

"Personal presence rules the world," Hale frequently stated when he was advising his friends to deliver introductions in person, particularly if they were soliciting funds. Mr. John D. Rockefeller, he told one man, would never see his appeal for money if it came through the mail and if a clerk had opportunity to throw it away. Letters on behalf of various friends were addressed by Hale to A. P. Stanley, the dean of Westminister Cathedral; to the Reverend Samuel G. May; to Richard Watson Gilder; even to "any friends" in California, on behalf of Miss Minna Smith, an otherwise unidentified lady. An undated letter by Hale offers to introduce Edward Bellamy to John Brisben Walker, the publisher of the *Cosmopolitan Magazine*, who wanted to meet him.

Two letters to the Reverend W. H. Furness show the attention that Hale paid this kind of correspondence as early as 1850. One was written on behalf of a seventeen year old boy who was moving to Philadelphia and who needed encouragement and sympathy. Hale doubted that the boy would call on Furness, since he was under the supervision of an uncle who was both "pious" and "Presbyterian"—a combination uncooperative with liberal thought. Another letter to Furness, written on May 1, 1851, is the result of a commission to investigate the progress of a Harvard freshman, young Horace Furness, later the eminent editor of the Variorum Edition of Shakespeare. The son was doing very well, Hale reported in detail, sending his grades as recorded in the college office.

An example of Hale's courtesies to unknown correspondents is a letter from 1887 to "Dear Sir," an Englishman, now in the Buffalo and Erie County Public Library. In a seven page reply to questions, Hale discusses his preferences in the use of words. Sometimes he used letters of inquiry for published articles, such as a three thousand word reply to the question "Where Shall Polly Go to School?" (*Cosmopolitan*, XIII [May 1892]: 111–15).

Hale was not immune to disappointment nor above protesting real or imagined injuries to himself. His published letter that alleged incompetent proofreading in the *Atlantic* is similar in tone to his unpublished correspondence about other hazards of authorship: complaints about delayed printing and slow payment for his articles; press-work difficulties for his periodicals; the failure of publishing houses to sell his books or to report honestly on sales. In other letters, he resented newspaper attacks upon himself; he asked for the investigation of a plagiarist; and he indicated in 1887 that he was still hurt by the rejection of a story by *Blackwoods* in 1840. In expressions that range from melancholy acceptance to indignation or irritation, he reacted to the business world with gentlemanly but secular professionalism.[13]

Some of Hale's sharpest letters were intended for eventual publication, and one of these contains his purposely irritating assault on the speech habits of American women. It "made" the Boston *Post* (April 5, 1878) and the New York *Times* a few days later (April 8) through a planned disclosure by the recipient. Professedly commending this lady—a speech correctionist—Hale emphasized the shrill feminine yell then in vogue, a shriek or "clamor cry" used without differentiation, whether in making public speeches or summoning waiters.

In extreme contrast to such rare instances of reproof, Hale occasionally wrote out-and-out fan letters. His enthusiasm for Edwin Booth's portrayal of Hamlet is recorded in *Life and Letters* through a letter to the actor. Written on November 20, 1883, Hale acknowledges in it "how much you have added to my reverence for the play," which he and his family had attended the evening before. Not reprinted are an earlier letter that compliments Charlotte Cushman on a performance, and a much later one that thanks Minnie Maddern Fiske for her support of the Hale House social settlement and for her influence in a campaign for the prevention of cruelty to animals.

Hale's consideration for young writers was widely appreciated. One of the best known examples of Hale's assistance is Hamlin Garland's story in *Roadside Meetings* (1930).[14] A similar instance of encouragement was acknowledged by the Chicago novelist Henry B. Fuller, then the young author of *The Chevalier of Pensieri-Vani* (1890), who met Hale almost by chance and who was surprised at the warm greeting and appreciative reception he received.[15] In the same vein the journalist Edward P. Mitchell—later successor to Charles A. Dana on the New York *Sun*, but at the time a cub reporter in Boston—recalled Hale's friendly introduction of him as "a brother *Advertiser* reporter."[16]

Also characteristic of Hale's sponsorship of young talent is his reply in 1883 to an editor who had requested a Christmas story.

Hale had one, he wrote, which he would sell for one hundred dollars; but he recommended that the enquiring editor might prefer a story that Hale had received from a younger writer, which would be fresher than his own and less expensive. As an editor, Hale frequently analyzed the strength and weakness of manuscripts, even when he rejected them. A tactful letter of 1871 to a woman poet has been preserved; and another, written twenty years later, commends a volume of her poems and indicates the kind of long-maintained friendship that was typical of Hale.

CHAPTER 3

The Man Without A Country

I *Beginnings*

FEW stories have enjoyed as much fame as Hale's *The Man Without a Country*. Accepted by the public immediately upon its appearance in the *Atlantic Monthly* in 1863, this narrative was reprinted within the next year in both authorized and pirated book editions that sold a half million copies. Almost at once Philip Nolan, the remorseful exile, became as clearly defined a figure as Washington Irving's Rip Van Winkle or Ichabod Crane; and he was more recognizable as an American character than the protagonists or the antagonists of Hawthorne's or Poe's tales. As a combination of immediate success and enduring emotional relevance, it is unique among American stories written for magazines. Its reputation as a minor classic was honestly earned, for it is the result of solid craftsmanship as well as of a spontaneous identification with the emotional needs of a deeply disturbed reading public.

For Hale, the success of *The Man Without a Country* was indeed major. In addition to marking the peak of his literary success, it was the foundation of his future celebrity and of his success in activities far removed from the writing of popular fiction. To the public at large, he was "author" of *The Man Without a Country* rather than an eminent preacher, an earnest reformer, or an indefatigable journalist. Without the tremendous success of his best seller, whose title was itself magic during the remainder of Hale's life, he would probably have been no more a sage and seer than his good friends Henry Bellows, James Freeman Clarke, W. H. Furness, or other Unitarian ministers who were recognized as men of ability and accomplishment within their profession and denomination.

Hale's three first published stories appeared in the *Boston Miscellany* in 1842. They were followed by more, infrequently and uneventfully, in other magazines; but these publications lacked lasting success until the characteristic ingenious yarn "My Double and How He Undid Me" appeared in the September 1859 *Atlantic Monthly*. His second story for this magazine—not his second contribution—was the famous patriotic expression, in December 1863. Although nothing in his earlier work foreshadowed its sensational success, the basic craftsmanship of its construction followed twenty years of practice and experience.

The narrative core of *The Man Without a Country* is a simple anecdote, which readers vividly recall from their youthful acquaintance and which literary handbooks have had no difficulty compressing within a few sentences. A young army officer convicted of treason angrily expresses the hope that he may never again hear the name of his native country: "Damn the United States. I wish I may never hear of the United States again!" As his penalty, his wish is granted by the court; he spends the remainder of his life at sea, is transferred from one government ship to another, and is tortured by incessantly intensifying remorse. The development of two sentences into ten thousand words of inspirational narrative called into existence all of Hale's latent ability in finding and arranging the details of a convincing story. The unprecedented popular success, not duplicated in forty more years of Hale's authorship, depended on circumstances beyond his control.

Some of these details need to be reviewed freshly to give a clearer idea of Hale's initial accomplishment. Throughout the story, he is very lenient toward his unfortunate young man, whose first transgression was hardly important. Philip Nolan had been reared on the wild frontier of Texas, surrounded by the plots and counterplots of intriguing Frenchmen and Spaniards. His irregular education, pieced together from private British tutors and by association with foreign commercial interests, had lacked the moral discipline to temper the swagger of an impatient aristocratic youth. Though outwardly a fine young army lieutenant, he easily fell prey to the wily Aaron Burr and his imperialistic schemes. Nolan was no doubt guilty of disloyalty because he was naive and foolish—not because of his ineradicable criminality.

In the treason trials of 1807 which followed at Richmond and elsewhere, Aaron Burr himself and other principals escaped conviction; but poor little Nolan, as Hale called him, was caught in the bureaucratic net. His penalty should not have been and might not have been severe except for his profane and seditious outburst as his trial was drawing to a close. His imprisonment on the *Levant*—his permanent place of confinement except when the vessel arrived in home ports—was due to his rejection of the Union, the *United* States; and his crime was secession—divisiveness to the same degree, in principle, as the desertion to the Confederacy of General Braxton Bragg or General Pierre Gustav Toutant de Beauregard, "who broke a soldier's oath two years ago [before 1863]," or of the great oceanographer Matthew Fontaine Maury, who broke a sailor's.[1]

Once young Nolan had been placed aboard ship, treated with all outward respect and with as much humaneness as his extraordinary punishment permitted, he was forgotten by the Washington bureaucracy. He became officially a cipher, a mysterious nonperson known to his companions by the fanciful nicknames of the "Man in the Iron Mask," or the unidentified political pamphleteer "Junius" or, usually, "Plain-buttons," to whom even the most petty insignia of his native land were denied. During fifty years, Nolan bore this burden of absolute exile; he grew in wisdom and moral strength; but he suffered horribly for his impulsive rejection of the *United* States. In 1863, the topical references were as vital to Hale's purpose as the contrived sequence of events.

In the course of time, Hale printed several accounts of the origin of his story that contain, in spite of minor discrepancies, as complete a commentary about its antecedents as it has received.[2] In fact, instigations of his sources were numerous. The most immediate origin was Hale's invitation from the *Atlantic Monthly* for patriotic opposition to the Secessionists in the dark days of 1863 when the outcome of the war between the states was still in doubt. Stimulation of a different kind was Hale's long-standing speculation that the British might have better handled Napoleon after Waterloo had they not exiled him to St. Helena. This view was the outcome of Hale's reading Walter Scott's biography of Napoleon and other contributions to the Napoleonic legend.

Hale's fusion of these sources was effected by the political eloquence of Clement Laird Vallandigham of Ohio, a Peace Democrat and Copperhead who had expressed such violent dislike of Abraham Lincoln and the Republican administration that he was banished to the Confederacy. He did not choose to remain there; and, after his return to the North, he was a candidate in 1863 for political office in

Ohio. Both Walter Scott and Vallandigham play their parts in Hale's story: the former, through quotation of the famous lines on patriotism from *The Lay of the Last Minstrel;* the latter, through a warning to all rash extremists "of what it is to throw away a country."

Hale believed he had the promise of the *Atlantic* editor to put the story in print before the November elections, but publication was probably delayed because the manuscript reached the magazine too late for the October or November issues rather than because of the editorial negligence of which Hale complained. By December, Vallandigham had lost the election; and, as a result of delay of publication, Hale had been deprived, as he says, of the illusion that he had contributed to the defeat.

The last easily identifiable basis for Hale's creation of his story is his often-expressed attitude, inherent since his Federalist boyhood, toward the Aaron Burr conspiracy and the weakness of the Jeffersonian party. For a story of sedition, the shady dealings of Burr were as inevitable a beginning as the Civil War was an ending; therefore the dates were chosen as 1807 (September 23) for the sentencing of Hale's fictional antihero and as 1863 (May 11) for Nolan's death. Hale read as many histories, memoirs, and newspapers as he could get during the summer to create a factual background whose verisimilitude could not be questioned. At the same time he was so determined that the plot would be totally fictional that he read the complete Navy Department reports from 1798 to 1861 so "that I might be sure of local color, that I might never, by any accident, place a vessel in the place where she really was, or name an officer so that a real man could be annoyed."

Hale's documentation, so complete that even some military officials mistook his fiction for fact, failed in one of the most important details of all fiction writing—his character's name. "Philip Nolan," his final selection, which he believed he had invented, was instead the actual name of a local Texas hero who had been shot by the Spaniards in 1801 at Waco. Hale had read about Nolan in garbled accounts from which he had not realized the man's importance, and he had somehow remembered him inaccurately as "Stephen Nolan." His own imaginary Nolan was intended to be a brother or cousin of the historical Nolan; but, through this almost inexplicable lapse of memory, the hero's name had been given to a traitor. The tremendous continued popularity of the story turned attention to even such a small discrepancy as a confusion over names, and Hale's concern with apologies and reparations occupied him to the end of his life.

After such systematic, almost pedantic preparation, it is remarkable how casual the story of Philip Nolan seems. Like the anecdote it is, the narrative is told in conversation by Frederic Ingham, one of Nolan's shipboard acquaintances. The side remarks, carefully alternating "this-I-know" with "this-I have-been-told," are in the best vein of oral narrative. Daniel Defoe has been cited as the model for Hale's convincing use of detail, but Hale deserves at least equal credit for his idiomatic speech rhythms. The stages of Nolan's awakened patriotism are quietly described without undue sentiment and even such an episode as an encounter with a Portuguese slave ship is in keeping with the fundamental appeal to national unity. Hale's primary target in 1863, like Lincoln's at that time, was secession; but Hale recognized that slavery was an interwoven cause of the war. Until the last pages of *The Man Without a Country*, this outgrowth of war hysteria is one of the least hysterical productions of the period. Although the story does not promise the Copperheads, even after their repentance, the joyful welcome due a returning prodigal son, neither does it threaten total damnation to the wicked.[3]

II *A Sequel:* Philip Nolan's Friends (1876)

Unlike most sequels, Hale's novel *Philip Nolan's Friends* was not written as the direct continuation of a literary success. Instead of being more of the same, it was an earnest attempt to make amends to the state of Texas and to the muse of history for the involuntary libel of *The Man Without a Country*. The attempt was not wholly successful. Texas may have been appeased by Hale's resolution to rescue the historical Nolan from "complete oblivion," as he explained in his preface; but the confusion between the two Philip Nolans, the imagined traitor and the regional patriotic hero, was not dispelled. Nor was history set straight by Hale's assertion that "no single day has done so much to make America strong, and to make Spain weak, as that day in 1801 when a Spanish officer, under his king's commission, murdered Philip Nolan"(5).[4] In keeping with such exaggeration, the rehabilitated Philip Nolan of the novel is a creature of romantic, idealized legend who is far removed from the one of historic records.[5]

The novel itself is a solidly constructed historical one of well over

a hundred thousand words, and it is written in the already out-
moded tradition of the British and American followers of Sir Walter
Scott. It's pattern resembles the romances of William Harrison
Ainsworth and G. P. R. James that had delighted Hale in his youth.
Pattern and substance both recall such old favorites as Cooper's *The
Spy* (1821), D. P. Thompson's *The Green Mountain Boys* (1839),
and, most of all, John Pendleton Kennedy's *Horse-Shoe Robinson*
(1835). A trace of Scott himself can be seen in one Silas Ransom—
whom Hale considered to be based upon the Hale family factotum,
Abel Fullum—a kindred soul to Caleb Balderstone in Scott's *The
Bride of Lammermoor* (1819).

Unlike most of Hale's longer fiction, *Philip Nolan's Friends* is
systematically plotted and is arranged to provide genuine suspense
as well as artificial complications. The narrative combines a
documented historical and geographical background that is interpreted with unashamed patriotic fervor, and conventional romances
that culminate in marriages amidst general rejoicing. The elements
of private and public welfare are carefully interwoven, and an ample
variety of incidents satisfied the old-fashioned readers for whom it
was intended.

Approximately the first third is a detailed narrative of the dangerous journey of two American ladies from New Orleans to San Antonio in 1800 when both Louisiana and Texas were controlled by
Spain and when the governors hated each other quite as heartily as
they hated Frenchmen and Americans. Much of the land was desert
territory occupied by roaming bands of Indians and by wild animals
almost as cruel as the savage Indians and Mexicans. The second
third of the book describes the relatively civilized life of the ladies in
the San Antonio of 1801, and their existence contrasts to the brutal
enslavement or murder of American traders in the unsettled parts of
Texas. After a return to New Orleans by boat, the ladies survive the
complicated intrigue of the French and Spanish bureaucrats; and,
through a combination of their own courage and the achievements of
American diplomacy, they achieve the happiness they have earned.

The two ladies are Inez Perry, age seventeen, and her Aunt
Eunice, age thirty-five. Their constant companion is a family servant, Silas Ransom, a determined Yankee, poor in book learning but
rich in dialect. Despite the role of Silas, Philip Nolan is the ladies'
friend and their best guide during much of their dreadful trip to San
Antonio. Of more importance to Hale, he is the ideal American hero

whose treacherous murder, which occurs barely past the midpoint
of the book, foreshadows the heroism of the Alamo and the eventual
addition of Texas to the great American Empire. With Nolan is a
younger man of similar merit, Will Harrod, who escapes from
Spanish captivity and survives to marry Inez.

To chart the plot of *Philip Nolan's Friends* in detail would be an
unprofitable enterprise; and to analyze the characters, either friends
or villainous foes, would be equally unprofitable. Inez is all sweet-
ness, immature and youthfully pert, but brave and clever. Eunice is
mature, self-composed, but brave and clever as well. Ransom, a
true Yankee, is loyal, self-reliant, humorous, brave, and extremely
clever. Only "White Hawk" or "Ma-ry"—a white girl who had been
kidnapped in the cradle by Apaches and who is rescued on the route
to San Antonio—shows any complexity or depth as she emerges
from the barbarism of her captors and resumes her rightful American heritage. The enemies, whether Indians, Spaniards, or "greas-
ers," are enemies, nothing more.

Other aspects of the book are worthier of attention. The description of the country is admirably expressed if the reader conquers his
antipathy toward the author's expansionist enthusiasm. The
dialogue is relatively natural, on the whole, and many episodes are
told simply, with an almost epic economy and reserve. In Philip
Nolan's final battle, when he and his companions are hopelessly
outnumbered, "not ten minutes after the sharp-shooting began,
Nolan exposed himself too fearlessly, was struck by a ball in the
head and fell dead, without a word"(237).

Aside from Hale's primary desire to make amends for his over-
sight in having used a hero's name for a traitor, his purpose in
writing *Philip Nolan's Friends* was educational. He had discovered
that the more he had studied the documents of Texas history the
more he wished to impress the American public with its importance
to the growth of the nation. The result led to a second subtitle that is
more educational than the original "Show Your Passports"—*A Story
of the Change of Western Empire.* As this subtitle indicates, he
glimpsed the significance of a moving frontier a generation before
Frederick Jackson Turner's brilliant professional theorizing. In
thinking about Texas, Hale recalled with considerable satisfaction
his youthful unsuccessful effort as a pamphleteer to save the new
state from slavery. To verify his impressions of the region and to
eliminate possible errors in describing it, he toured from New Or-

leans to San Antonio and beyond in 1875; in fact, he desired to assure himself of the accuracy of his description of the country between San Antonio and the Gulf of Mexico as "one of the loveliest of the world"(267).

In minor ways, Hale's abiding interest in fiction as a vehicle for general education is manifest. He frequently pauses to define unusual meanings of words like *opportunity*(14), *bosman*(21), *smoking-halt*(26), *filibuster*(84), *voiture* and *galliot*(304), and *mustang*(339). When he quotes a song of the times, he also includes the music to give his readers the opportunity of performing it(26). Most important is a lengthy description of Indian sign language and hieroglyphics that he introduces with apparently unnecessary detail(67–68), but he makes this material essential in regard to the rescue of White Hawk, who knows no English and who without signs would have prevented Hale's happy conclusion.

A rudimentary theory of history connects the incidents, and Hale's essential concept of the historic process is the cause-and-effect relationship of individual actions. "From Phil Nolan came Salcedo's madness," the peroration begins (Salcedo was the Spanish governor). "From their frightened dispatches home, came the easy gift of all this country to France. . . . Philip Nolan never was afraid. He has done more for his country than he meant. . . . Nolan's mad act has given Louisiana to your country; it will give her Texas"(395).

Patriotic fervor is more obvious, however, than an acceptance without condescension of racial or international differences. Inez is portrayed as a model of girlish virtue, although she is once characterized as an "exaggerated American"(220) whose raillery against the English is caused not only by her veneration of Washington and Franklin but also by her ignorance of "the littlenesses of their countrymen"(220). This mild reproof undoubtedly extends to the exaggerated patriotism of Ransom, the homesick Puritan who carries his documentary record of American citizenship next to his heart but whose unbridled language emphasizes his prejudices: "Niggers is bad; French folks is bad; English is wus; and Spanish is wus than them, by a long sight; but redskins is the wust on 'em all. They's lazy, that's one thing; so is the mounseers. They's proud as the Devil, that's one thing; so is the Englishmen. They'll lie 's fast 's they can talk: so'll the Spaniards; 'n' they'll cheat and steal, and pretend they can't understand nothing' you say all the time. They's a bad set"(244).

III *Hale's Additions*

Philip Nolan's Friends, though readable, could never be rated as a major novel. Its import—the complacent assertion of American superiority—makes the poor substitute of imperialist pride for the deeply felt patriotic anxiety of *The Man Without a Country*. Nonetheless, Hale's concern over Nolan did not end. New editions of the 1863 story stimulated new introductions, notably in 1897 and 1898, without basic changes. As late as 1901 Hale wrote the introduction to a Spanish court record that was printed by the Mississippi Historical Society, and he contributed an even later afterthought about the log of Nolan's prison ship to the *National Geographic*. [6]

How many anthologies included *The Man Without a Country* is mere speculation, as is also the number of translations. In addition to conventionally printed trade editions, it appeared in Pitman, Graham, and Gregg shorthand; in braille; and as a comic paperback. Numerous inexpensive school editions with suitably educational introductions[7] are accompanied by a patriotic edition sponsored by the Veterans of Foreign Wars and an expensive illustrated volume for the Limited Editions Club (1936) with an introduction by Carl Van Doren. It has been recited on phonograph records; and it has been rewritten for radio programs and, as late as 1973, for a national television network. Although it has been staged as a one act play, it has also been published by Samuel French as a play in three acts, prologue, and epilogue. A commercial moving picture was made in Hollywood, and an operatic version was composed by Walter Damrosch and was sung at the Metropolitan Opera.

None of the theatrical adaptations of *The Man Without a Country* was successful, perhaps because none of them was particularly good because they lacked the balance of theme and form achieved initially by Hale. The theme itself has been both approved and disapproved in varying degrees. Years ago the story was acclaimed as "the best sermon on patriotism ever written."[8] a well-intended compliment that backfired late in the century into condemnation of this work as "the primer of jingoism."[9] The explanation of such discrepancy between rhetorical superlatives is found in military history, not in gross ambiguity in Hale's story. His close friend Thomas Wentworth Higginson, who pronounced it "capital" in 1863, feared in 1898 that it inclined toward jingoism; for Higginson was a Union army officer during the Civil War and an anti-imperialist during the Spanish-American War.

Though no chauvinist, Hale was inclined at times to emphasize the immediate political purpose of his fable at the expense of its value as a creative expression. Never a pacifist, he did not equate love of country with military aggressiveness. He had disapproved of the American attack on Mexico in 1845, contrary to the implications of *Philip Nolan's Friends* thirty years later; and, at his most militaristic, he lacked the customary swagger and bluster of the true jingoist. As a man of peace, if not of peace at any price, he was more "hawk" than "dove," yet less of a hawk than most enthusiasts are during a war of which they approve. Hale himself had no doubts of the justness of the Northern cause in the Civil War, for he viewed the Southern appeal to separatism as a repudiation of the Revolution no less than of the Constitution. Since he was an unwavering supporter of President Lincoln and the national union, his story was, as had been observed, a direct assault upon secession; and, compared to this aspect, its other contents and values were secondary in 1863.

In war as in peace, Hale was generally a practical man, a realist. Of his four Civil War poems, two encouraged enlistments and two the purchase of government bonds *(Works*, X, 73–79). "Take the Loan" opens with Yankee realism:

> Come, freemen of the land,
> Come meet the great demand,
> True heart and open hand,—
>   Take the loan!
> For the hopes the prophets saw,
> For the swords your brothers draw,
> For liberty and law,
>   Take the loan![10]

Hale's support of the Civil War bonds also took in such other forms as articles for the *Advertiser*, a sermon on the religious duty of subscribing, and the promotion of a musical performance of his verses. When reprinting "Take the Loan" in his *Works* (X, 74), he added, as of October 1900: "Written [1861] when people had to be persuaded as patriots to subscribe for a 7.30 loan! Those who did so are today's millionaires." Hale himself had not profited from an 1861 investment; he had more zeal for the Union cause than money.

Diminishing as the appeal to critics and readers of *The Man Without a Country* has been, its appearance of photographic realism continues to convince persons of nonliterary appreciation. Hale's myth can easily be misjudged and broadened to include the draft-dodger, the impenitent fugitive from justice, the criminal deservedly in solitary confinement, or any vaguely antisocial subversive. That such characters are not true to Hale's text is less important to an indignant citizen that that each is or ought to be "a man without a country." "What this country needs today," wrote a retired Marine Corps officer in 1968, is a "Philip Nolan Law." Such a law would "recognize such deliberate acts [as Nolan's] as a voluntary and deliberate renunciation of U.S. citizenship" for which a fitting penalty would be permanent exile. The officer grouped deserters with draft-dodgers (neither of which Nolan was) who journeyed to Japan or to Sweden or who skipped "across the Canadian border to evade their duty."[11]

Like other effective symbols, Hale's imagined Philip Nolan can easily be made the source of inferences remote from the creator's original purpose; but some extensions of meaning are appropriate or at least plausible. As a recent editor has observed, minimizing Hale's didacticism and looking beyond the immediate theme of loyalty or patriotism, the story reveals on a deeper symbolic level "man's psychological need for identity and involvement with institutions." Approached in the social tradition of Aristotle's "man is by nature a political animal" and of John Donne's "no man is an island," Hale's story remains "highly relevant in this modern age in which questions of legal and moral dissent abound."[12]

Such a restatement is by no means incongruous, for Hale was identifying himself with the object of his pity and was also pleading for reconciliation, not for retaliatory punishment. His Philip Nolan was, as its worst, his interpretation of a naive youth and not of a deliberate traitor like Benedict Arnold or a Satanic schemer like Aaron Burr. Philip Nolan was, in fact, a victim misled by faulty rearing through which, "in a word, to him 'United States' was scarcely a reality"—a statement that describes too well a situation existent today. Apart from its political theme appropriate to 1863, Hale's story is also a religious parable. More orthodox in its implications than Hale's denominational liberalism, it parallels man's fall; his alienation from righteousness; his reconversion and repentance; his eventual pardon and salvation.

CHAPTER 4

. . . And Other Stories

I Preliminaries

HALE'S short stories, rather than his longer fiction, remain his liveliest and most readable literary productions. Written between 1842 and 1897, they number about a hundred. After the original periodical publication for which they were designed, the majority, starting in 1868, were gathered into eight collections; others were sold as separate booklets; but only about twenty-five of them were selected for inclusion in the ten volume set of *Works* (1898–1900). However, several reasons make such exact figures impractical because some of Hale's short "stories" are less fiction than fact and because some are less "short" than middle length. The most important consideration for Hale was frequently the number of pages needed for the next issue of a magazine, and he was more likely to pad an anecdote than to truncate an organic plot. The same editorial expediency influenced the appearance among his collected short stories of a few factual narratives and contemplative essays, and his translations of *Nicolette and Aucassin* from the French and "The Queen of California" from the Spanish.

Except for Hale's first attempts—ones deserving special attention in a writer's career—a classification of his short fiction by theme or style is more significant than by chronology. The two main types are represented by the best known titles: predominantly humorous anecdotes like "My Double and How He Undid Me" (1859) and basically serious fables such as "The Man Without a Country" (1863). This distinction is only moderately helpful since most of his humorous tales develop a serious purpose. From first to last, his idea of the function of fiction was the Classical, Roman combination of instruction and entertainment; but Hale lacked any clear method of subordinating one to the other. His expression of his intention is found in a Christian paraphrase: he referred to "high authority for teaching by parable," and he added that, "whatever else people will read or will not read, they do read short stories, on the whole, more than they read anything else."[1]

As a professional writer, Hale worked from literary models rather than from theories; and, as a result, some of his early pieces are as definitely structured and as highly unified as those of Nathaniel Hawthorne or Edgar Allan Poe; others are as loosely constructed as those published in the family magazines. Hale believed that the most important embellishment for short fiction was the light touch for which editors never cease to search; and, whenever he was annoyed by readers who considered humorous tales unministerial, he reminded them that he had a supply of 1096 sermons to which in 1880 he was regularly adding one a week, with "some few . . . for sale in print."[2]

In his short fiction Hale utilized recurrent themes and mannerisms that distinguished his work from that of other practicing writers of his time. Among these were flights into pure whimsicality; a fondness for Christmas tales, modernized versions of Classical literature, and tales of travel; addiction to the framework device, including the creation of an alter ego in one of his characters, Frederic Ingham; excursions into science fiction; a permanent campaign for the protection of privacy; and repeated illustrations of the conviction that actions, trivial in themselves, initiate chain reactions of unpredictable complexity.

Hale's earliest published stories were three which, after failing to sell them elsewhere, he reluctantly contributed to his brother's *Boston Miscellany* in 1842. As experiments in varied attitudes, they reveal a serious interest in commercial writing. The first to appear, the vaguely allegorical "A Tale of A Salamander," had few successors; the second, "Love by the Way," was a poor performance; but the third, "The South American Editor," was definitely in the manner of his later humorous sketches. Based upon his experience on the staff of the *Advertiser,* this third story mixes descriptions of journalistic and political chaos with an intentionally absurd chain of incidents concerning an attempted elopement and reaching an ideally happy ending through which his young journalist, George Hackmatack, wins prosperity, a sweetheart, and an opportunity to reappear in Hale's stories for the following forty years.

"Love by the Way; or, What Happened to Me," another preposterous anecdote, is less amusing, mainly because it is as unnecessarily wordy throughout as its title. The narrator, a self-satisfied youth, is so talkative that he fails to notice that the beautiful girl to whom he proposes marriage, after two days' acquaintance, is deaf and dumb. Both the narrative core and the setting, a stagecoach trip in New England, foreshadow Hale's later work; but the satire is smothered for the reader by the narrator's comments.

Hale's earliest printed story, "A Tale of a Salamander," is a symbolic, ambivalent fable that contains many of Nathaniel Hawthorne's characteristics. The central character, a tremendous student—but of what branch of learning is not disclosed—has been fascinated by the insistence of glassblowers in a neighborhood factory that the fires be put out every forty days. Otherwise, the workmen believe, a salamander will emerge. "Is this possible?" the young man asks himself; "will a salamander actually emerge? Will it be malignant or friendly? Will it be subhuman or intelligent and capable of communication?" In the spirit of Christopher Marlowe's Faustus, Hale's modern youth, dreaming of himself as another Isaac Newton or Robert Fulton, asks the naively selfish question of how the production of a salamander from a fire, which he has come to believe is more than likely, will entitle him to fame and glory. His questions are never answered, for his forty day fires are extinguished three times, on the last day, by the chance intervention of Mrs. Mumler, his landlady. The sole result of his experiments is a violent fever that is followed by a return to sense.

Hale provided no precise statement of his meaning. When the youth's friend, mildly curious about the glassblowers' tradition, wonders if there may not be more than superstition to the myth of the salamander, the student, "ghastly pale and almost fainting," implores him to seek no further: "Don't try it! . . . The only gratification my trial has left me is the ability it has given me to warn my friends against following my example."[3]

The unresolved conclusion of "A Tale of a Salamander" has few successors among Hale's mature stories. Its ambiguity may have been purely a literary experiment, yet it may have been a reminder to him, in the spasmodic turbulence of youth, that self-restraint should guide even the search for knowledge.

During the fifteen years that followed the short life of the *Boston Miscellany*, Hale had no assured outlet for short stories or narrative-descriptive sketches. The four preserved stories first appeared in such diverse publications as the *Monthly Religious Magazine* of Boston; *Sartain's*—a family type magazine; the Hale family's *Advertiser;* and a religious anthology that he himself edited. Among them, "The Last Voyage of the Resolute" appears to be a factual journalistic account of Arctic exploration; two are religious sketches of only secondary narrative interest; but none of the four shows any special talent for fiction or points to Hale's later success with the genre.

"The Old and the New, Face to Face" shows Nero judging Paul: "Faith on the one side, before expediency and cruelty on the other."[4] In "A Piece of Possible History" the rivals, Homer and David, are more evenly matched; but the Hellenic champion, lacking the true God, fails to equal the Psalmist. The remaining sketch, "Friends' Meeting" is a tentative stream-of-consciousness reverie unusual for 1848 and is an experiment in writing that Hale did not pursue further: "Some one spoke! No, it was the moving door which startled me. I hope it will not swing to. I must see still that shadow of the branch flitting to and fro on the outer wall there. What a handwriting it is! So graceful! and with every new motion so different from that before! beautiful, and infinite, like all the rest! Must these inner walls around us be left so bare, and coldly white, and unornamental?"[5] Has the unknown thinker, so sensitive to nature and the manmade church, hinted in this last sentence at a blemish in the Quaker religious service which a portion of Hellenism could remove?

II *Map Peddlers and Other Nuisances*

With "My Double and How He Undid Me," Hale's first story for the *Atlantic Monthly,* he began a successful career as a writer with a recognized individual style and subject. This very amusing story, ingenious as it is, was more than a good joke. A summary of the conflicting claims of society and solitude, it marked the opening of Hale's lifelong campaign for the preservation of privacy; for this narrative epitomizes a dilemma from which Hale, a man of surpassingly good will, never extricated himself: the citizen's need to participate and the individual's need to escape. Although none of his fictional successors with this theme has had the appeal of "My Double and How He Undid Me"—which for years was the only story by Hale, except "The Man Without a Country," that was widely anthologized or continuously in print—these stories suggest as a group many defenses that good citizens can use against unwelcome appeals for money or time.

The story itself, as narrated by the Reverend Frederic Ingham, recalls a happy year in which he imagined he had solved the problem of both participating and escaping. Disgusted with quasi-civic duties that interfere with his vocation, the minister trains an illiterate, who resembles him amazingly, to substitute for him at inane meetings where only his presence is required. Dennis Shea, the double, is harmless, amiable, and patient; and he is taught four responses to requests that carry him through an entire year without detection: "Very well, thank you. And you?. . . . I am very glad you like it. . . . There has been so much said, and, on the whole, so well said, that I will not occupy the time. . . . I agree, in general, with my friend on the other side of the room." Eventually the use of a substitute is discovered when Shea fumbles his clichés, and Ingham is forced to flee to the Maine wilderness to begin life anew.

Another of Hale's ministers, in a story written many years later, solved the problem of overexposure more successfully, more economically, and more honestly than Ingham. "The Minister's Black Veil," one of Hale's numerous stories of literary origin, is less an imitation of Nathaniel Hawthorne than a reproof;[6] and its subtitle, "With Full Particulars," is a reference to original documents that Hawthorne allegedly had suppressed in writing his *Twice-Told Tales*. According to Hale's thrice-told version, the veil was dark blue; and it was only one of a number in various colors that Mr. Hooper's lively sister-in-law had sewed into his hats to give him privacy as he walked out of doors. Mr. Hawthorne made too much of a mystery of what was a practical expedient for avoiding interruptions, and the result was that Mr. Hooper's sermons were much improved by the time he saved in preparing them.[7]

In Hale's "His Level Best," a warning against compliance, the narrator, unlike Frederic Ingham and Mr. Hooper, never attempts to escape. As Hale wrote, in mock seriousness, Mr. Boothby was "an unfortunate gentleman, now resident in the poorhouse" because he ignored "the absurdity of the pressure which some of the organizations of society make upon the best of its individual members." The account of how Boothby squandered his resources is humorous, but the peroration is serious: "Hold to the level best which the commonplace of society demands of you, and you come out on the quagmire flat of the dismal swamp of worthless indecision" (*Works*, I, 163).

Another amusing yarn, one of Hale's last on the escape theme, is "Colonel Clipsham's Calendar." The colonel himself, a popular speaker at useless meetings, was much in demand for such organizations as the Consolidated Sodality of Lovers of Art, the Soul of the Soldiery, the Brothers in Adversity, the Carriage-Builders' Association, and the Friends of Good Government. Confusing his dates, he delivered a routine college speech to the Grand Army of the Republic, and the alumni mistakenly received a speech for the carriage makers. Because the colonel had so successfully eliminated the platitudes of the past which bored his audiences, he was elected governor without a campaign.

In "The Happy Island," the problem of public nuisances is solved forever. The wealthy and public-spirited Crapsten is induced by friends to leave home for a summer of seclusion from the pesterers who had been absorbing his time: "Map-Peddlers had long been the generic term in that family for that immense class of people who, in the present form of our civilization, come in upon you, with no claim whatever, to grind their own axes or advance their own interests, without the least regard to your convenience or to any of your rights" (*Works*, I, 366). During Crapsten's absence, his mad "conspirators" of friends intercepted each week twenty to thirty such map-peddlers and shipped them all—reformers, propagandists, or salesmen alike—to an island off the coast of Florida. By winter they had assembled a population of nearly a hundred individuals who were supported from Crapsten's wealth and who were perfectly happy doing nothing but harangue each other.

Viewing these stories as a group, one finds in them the struggle, if it can be called so, between intelligence and folly, not between good and evil. Hale's Boston world harbored no villains and few rascals, contained many men of good will, and had an approximately equal number of gulls. As Hale well knew, he was an inveterate map-peddler himself; for, in addition to joining and commending redundant societies for preserving tradition or promoting progress, he found time to sign and disseminate petitions, to offer prayer at memorial services, and to preside at the dedication of boys' clubs and at Republican political rallies. As early as 1857, he was circulating printed appeals for donations to the publication fund of the American Antiquarian Society. As late as 1904, he was lobbying strenuously in Washington for improved copyright protection—an effort that produced one hundred dollars each from his two friends, Howells and Mark Twain. Between times, he was raising funds for

Antioch College in Ohio, for preservation of the Old South Meeting House in Boston, for Afro-American education at Hampton Institute, and for many other benevolences.

Along with such multitudinous appeals for help in improving the world, Hale was a genuine humorist with the grace to see himself as a member of the human race in its less attractive as well as in its most constructive activities; and map-peddling was only one among many such occupations. Thus in "Round the World in a Hack," a tribute to Boston, he laughed at himself as a Bostonian. As an enthusiastic tourist, he learned how to ridicule travelers as a class in his presentation of the silly Englishman of "The Modern Sindbad" and of the sightseers in "Cromwell's Statue" who failed to notice that a statue of Oliver Cromwell had been substituted in Westminster Hall for one of Charles II. He sniped at the literary life as freely as at his own other addictions; and he did so successfully in "Alif-Laila," a satire on magazine serials, and in "John Rich and Lucy Poor," a comic dream-fullfillment story—one based on his own productiveness—in which a lover wrote a million words a month to persuade his sweetheart's father that the production of literature could be a gainful occupation.

A type of story on which Hale repeatedly exercised his wit was modernized and revised versions of old favorites. Hale's results varied, ranging from an impressive imitation of Defoe to a depressing failure with Shakespeare. "Crusoe in New York," an extremely ingenious stylistic copy of its model, is lightly humorous in its contrast of fact and fiction; but it is serious as a criticism of urban life in which isolation like that of a desert island is possible. In "Both Their Houses," an irreverent parody of a Shakespearean classic, the American hero is Romayne Montague, the heroine is Juliet Hood, and the Reverend Mr. Lawrence is the Presbyterian minister who marries them. Hale's version has no Tybalt, no Mercutio, no murders, no deaths, and no excitement; for, as Hale observed, "It may be observed here that one difficulty which the American novelist has in creating a plot for his country which would pass muster in Europe is, that the greater part of his countrymen and women do not act like sheer fools in delicate or difficult circumstances. Now half the received plots require action of this sort, or there is no story. This observation, thrown out by a friend of the court, is commended to the critics."[8]

Today's reader can take Hale's lightweight fooling or leave it, according to his mood; but he can respond more easily to the circumstances of stories like "A Civil Servant" in which the development is less different from that in this world. Although humorous in both intention and accomplishment, this tale is a bitter satire—bitter, that is, for Hale—about the parasitic bureaucrat John Sapp who has been trained to do nothing in particular, wants to do nothing, and is therefore fitted only for a job in which nothing is to be done. After applying unsuccessfully for twenty such fine government offices as county surveyor (duties done by proxy), Sapp receives an appointment to an uninhabited island in the Aleutians where he becomes utterly mad and completely happy.

III *Frederic Ingham and Other Doubles*

By all odds the most fully realized of Hale's fictional characters is Frederic Ingham, who was originally invented as the narrator of magazine stories for which the anonymity of authors was the rule. In this capacity, Ingham served as the harassed minister of "My Double and How He Undid Me" and as the naval officer who was friend and confidant of Philip Nolan in *The Man Without a Country*. As Hale continued to use the name in other tales and anecdotes, Ingham developed into both a transparent nom de plume and a man of amazingly varied experiences and aptitudes. For Hale's second collection of magazine fiction, *The Ingham Papers* (1869)—ten pieces, several of which had been attributed to Ingham—Hale provided a parody prefatory "memoir" that is a model of his mock-serious humor.

"It is always difficult to write the biography of the living," he began; but it is "more difficult to write the biography of a friend." More intimately than that, Hale stated that "I have shared his thoughts, his purse, his confidence," and "shared in the same adventure"(vii). The biography ends, after a dozen pages, with a promise of later papers by Ingham, captain, U.S.N., sometime pastor of the First Sandemanian Church in Naguadavick, and major-general by Brevet in the Patriotic Service in Italy. This promise was kept many times in later short stories, in longer fiction, and in educational readings for children.

As early as 1869 Ingham was obviously the image of the man Hale would have liked to be. Part of his tribute to Ingham he later appropriated openly for himself: ". . . . Ingham was painfully conscious that he had no peculiar genius for one duty rather than another. If it were his duty to write verses, he wrote verses; to lay telegraph, he laid telegraph; to fight slavers, he fought slavers; to preach sermons, he preached sermons. And he did one of these things with just as much alacrity as the other; the moral purpose entirely controlling such mental aptness or physical habits as he could bring to bear"(xix). In time, Ingham attracted a circle of friends with whom he exchanged stories, and a group of children whose reading he guided. By 1885, he had aged into "a somewhat garrulous old gentleman" called Uncle Fritz who in a checkered, happy, useful life had accumulated wisdom and understanding in abundance.[9]

A significant clue to Ingham's meaning for Hale is the encompassing framework of the stories in the volume *Christmas in Narragansett* (1884). Long retired from military service and the ministry, the colonel had bought a summer home in the South—as far south as he could go in New England. As the book opens, the reader observes him on horseback while he is supervising the installation of a modern device, a telephone. It is a week before Christmas, and the colonel knows that his houseguests will need contact with the outside world. Sure enough, the telephone is no more than in place before the bell begins to ring. The guests arrive, and soon the winter season is in full swing at "Sybaris," in Narragansett, Rhode Island. A lively party gathers: old friends like the Haliburtons; newer friends like the Deckers; neighbors like the Hales. The weather is mild enough for outdoor sketching and hiking, but ample time remains for the storytelling in which Colonel Ingham takes the lead. Within this framework, Hale assembled thirteen stories, most of which had appeared in magazines during the preceding decade.

Although such inclusions in the collection may have been fortuitous, the arrangement and balance are more organic than in most of Hale's collections. The basic reason appears to have been the public discussions of the purpose of fiction stimulated by magazine articles by Anthony Trollope, Walter Besant, and Henry James. "Why do people love to hear or read stories? What is it all for?" the colonel's friends asked: "Is it that the reader may kill time? Is it that the author may reform the world, or save the reader's soul? Is it that the author may show you how well he can do it, as a skillful painter will copy for you a dry herring on a board? To these three questions— which represent the three theories—we tried to make the colonel give the answer"(83).

Hale's answer (for the colonel dodged the question) was to illustrate all three purposes. He included a large part of good fun, a dash or two of moral uplift, and a few gimmicks (not that they would have impressed Henry James) to illustrate his virtuosity. One of these last examples was a two page short-short transmitted to *Harper's* by telegraph. On another occasion, Hale confesses, he had observed that the Christmas issue of his magazine was instructive, wise, valuable, but dull. "There is yet no method known," he told his friends, "by which you can either inspissate [interject] entertainingness into a dull article—no—or varnish it with an entertaining copal [varnish]"(117). Therefore Hale wrote on the spot what he needed, "The Survivor's Story"—an eight page burlesque containing eight tall tales.

At another session the literary question under discussion was the differences between long and short fiction. There were facetious comments such as the condemnation of historical novels as written for people too lazy to read real history(285), but there was also a technical analysis of unity. As an editor, Colonel Ingham had read "thousands" of manuscripts in which "the condensation is put in at the wrong place"(110). An anecdote by Jo Miller could be expanded into a British three-decker, "but I think it is better," said the colonel, "to write a short story from which a long one can be evolved, than to write a long one which is to be cut down to so small a pattern"(112). To this comment, Hale added his own:

I said that it seemed to me that a short story was to be compared rather to a play than a novel. I should not insist on the Unities. I wrote a story once, of which the action covered nearly sixty years. But you must not, I think, have many characters; I think you must have no episodes; I doubt whether you may even have a double plot. If you want to marry off two or three accessory couples at the end, do so. But do not let their flirtations interfere with the play of the story.(116)

With this background of unaccustomed theory, Hale's stories in *Christmas in Narragansett* proceed as usual from pure entertainment, as Trollope prescribed, to the incitement to Christian duty, as Besant urged. The division is seldom complete, for no account of Judge Samuel Sewell, however it may concentrate on his daughter's romance, as in "The Governor's Dinner," can ignore the somber aspects of Puritan Massachusetts.

The invention of Frederic Ingham is not the only evidence of Hale's profound sense of human duplicates; for his stories abound in examples of people who look alike and of those who are alike but do not show it. Thus his fictional parallels are usually more than coincidences; the similarities between his characters are more than social conformity.' Although doubles sometimes undo a personality, they as frequently complete him. In the comic vein, "Law and Gospel" is a conceit about a Harvard University graduate student who cannot decide between law and the ministry as a career. He enrolls in both the law school, Tuesday-Thursday-Saturday, and divinity, Monday-Wednesday-Friday. For the divinity classes, he is G. Ernest Byram who wears black and spends his spare time teaching Sunday school. For law, he is dressed in the sporting clothes that are suitable to Boston society, and is George E. Byram. Nobody suspects that the two Byrams, although they look alike, are only one. When the girl who loves him as a divinity student repulses the student of law, Byram abandons his double life, his future decided for him.

Another kind of story of double personality, called "Colonel Ingham's Journey," recounts what the colonel himself described as a "philosophical experiment" and begins as a psychological fantasy and ends as an inconclusive mystical fable of Christian brotherhood. A wholly different worldly mood colors "A New Arabian Night," a sly bitterness toward upper level bureaucracy that goes beyond Hale's tolerant annoyance because of useless routine at the grassroots level. In this yarn, the president's death was kept secret until the end of his term; and an imposter—a professional Dromio—filled the position as well as the president did. "Times were prosperous," and, "as always, the country governed itself without much regard to Washington." The story first appeared in *Harper's Magazine* for March 1889, and is much more likely to have been a parting shot at Grover Cleveland than a foreboding relative to his Republican successor, Benjamin Harrison.

IV *The Utopian and the Fantastic*

A completely imagined Utopia needs a more solid base in recognizable fact than does an unrestrained fantasy. Hale tried both, but he sometimes fell into the errors of too explicit exhortation for reform or, at the other extreme, too whimsical elaboration of incredible customs and attitudes. More frequently, he succeeded; for he possessed the necessary concern for the public welfare, an essential experience with practical life, and the gift of irony. His most detailed Utopia, which is still pleasant reading, was originally a short serial in the *Atlantic* for 1868; for this narrative was too long for a single installment but not long enough for a novel. Published in 1869 as the major part of *Sybaris and Other Homes*, this story was supplemented by stories and articles about the evils of metropolitan congestion and about the need for housing reform. The added material included, "How They Lived at Naguadavick," a fictional sketch of the good life in an American small city of twenty-five to thirty-five thousand inhabitants, and factual accounts of wholesome living in Vineland (a small town near Philadelphia) and of unwholesome living and dying in Boston tenements. For the ninth volume of his collected works (1900), he added a longer piece, *How They Lived in Hampton*, first published in 1888. Thus the volume drew together his ideas, expressed both whimsically and earnestly, but indicated that his views had changed little in the course of thirty years. The writings vary in interest from the lively account of Sybaris to the plodding social blueprint of the Hampton community.[10]

The title sketch, "My Visit to Sybaris," follows the classic pattern established by Thomas More and Francis Bacon of a ship that finds shelter in an unexpected quarter and enables the narrator not only to observe an unknown society but to report about it to his fellow citizens. Hale's narrator is his old friend, Frederic Ingham, a gentleman of unquestioned probity, whose civic-mindedness prompts him to point out to his fellow citizens—and particularly to Bostonians—certain customs of Sybaris that might profitably be adapted to American cities.

The Sybaris of Hale's sketch is an ancient city on the Gulf of Tarentum that was once wealthy and famous for its luxury; was supposedly overthrown by enemies and razed in the sixth century B.C.; but was found not only existent, to Ingham's astonishment, in the midnineteenth century but flourishing in quiet isolation. This city has, one suspects, the charm of the Boston of Hale's youth, plus the conveniences of modern technology, but is denied the growing pains of industrialized urbanization. A city of small homes surrounded by gardens, Sybaris is a community in which the rights of the individual and of the public are equally protected and nurtured.

On the mechanical side, Sybaris is notable for its transportation facilities. It has horse railroads, with frequent service and no stand-

ees; cable cars for rapid transit that are privately owned but publicly
regulated; and steam wagons that must have looked like twentieth
century jeeps and that were more convenient than any vehicles in
the United States at the time. The telegraph, an invention of the
ancient Sybarites, provided an excellent intercommunication system.

Public utilities included laundries, bakeries, and umbrella stands.
Welfare was assured through pensions for everybody over sixty-five;
preferential employment opportunities existed for the handicapped;
simple church services were based on the Greek New Testament;
and there were small neighborhood theatres which had no professional actors. The government was democratic in that public officials
were elected to hold office indefinitely, until they resigned or were
recalled. Both men and women voted, unless they had refused to
serve in the military. Although neither crime nor poverty was unknown, each had been reduced to the minimum and presented no
growing problem. Foreign visitors, however uncommon, were
treated with great courtesy and entertained under the direction of a
special officer, a *proxenus*, as in ancient Athens.

The modern Sybarites lived simple lives, but tobacco was used
freely, except in public gatherings where it might annoy nonsmok-
ers. Wine was not forbidden. Sex meant marriage, which was compulsory for women by the age of twenty-five and for men by thirty,
unless the confirmed celibates preferred thirty years of exile. This
extreme penalty, Ingham discovered, was seldom if ever exacted;
but he refers to several cases of capital punishment for more serious
crimes, such as keeping people waiting for appointments or erecting
multistory buildings. The principles by which the Sybarites lived
are best expressed in Ingham's report: "With us [the *proxenus* told
him] the first object of the state, as an organization, is to care for the
individual citizen, be he man, woman, or child" (*Works*, IX, 53).
Like John Stuart Mill, as Ingham notes, "We try to see that each
individual is protected in the enjoyment, not of what the majority
likes, but of what he chooses, so long as his choice injures no other
man"(54). This individualism does not prevent families from
cooperating, if they prefer, in common kitchens, in playrooms for
children, and in libraries; but even so, "Robert Owen would hang
himself here"(78).

As Ingham describes Sybaris, it was an easy-going community; its
inhabitants are dedicated to comfort and relaxed living that is not

too plain and to thinking that is not too high. "I was never in a place," he says, "where there were so many tasteful pretty little conveniences for everybody"(58). Preferably a small city, it was not a great nation with international obligations. As one of the guides explained, "very little time is spent in legislation . . . there is not much account-keeping or litigation . . . and somehow everybody does his share of work"(65). Ingham also notes with pleasure that "as everybody serves somewhere"(85)—*everybody* being an indispensable word often used for describing this community—"everybody has plenty of time"(60).

Hale lacked the extreme Utopian faith in perfection. As a reformer, he foresaw an improvement in institutions; but he did not anticipate a revolution in human nature. "Ideals," a short story, is one of his most engaging sociological fables on this theme.[12] In it, four New England families, close friends, are discouraged by the deficiencies of American life and migrate to a perfect locality in Mexico. After an absolutely satisfactory winter, they return to New England, prepare for permanent emigration, and instead decide to remain there. The original complaints (itemized as Robinson Crusoe did his) were not trivial. As the Inghams said, "The country has gone to the dogs." The Haliburtons added, "People vote as if they were possessed." The Hackmatacks agreed, "How any man can live under this government I do not know." In the same vein the Carters noted "the increasing worthlessness of the franchise." In all, they had found twenty-four grounds for complaint, none of which existed in primitive Mexico; but, even so, the irresistible appeal of the native land won the day. They returned wiser, not sadder; for whatever they could not try to cure, they decided, they could ignore.

As a whimsical successor to "My Visit to Sybaris," another short *Atlantic Monthly* serial, "The Brick Moon" (1869), continues the play with Utopian fancies; but this tale is more obviously science fiction. Not only the first story ever written about an artificial earth satellite, it is the longest one that deals mainly with this subject until 1953; and, according to a historian of science fiction, it is a prophetic work.[12] Unaware of this distinction as a pioneer, Hale used his curiosity about physical science to heighten his readers' interest in his appeal for right living. The narrator, a participating observer but not an astronaut, was again Frederic Ingham; but, on this occasion, his function is that of an amateur scientist.

The satellite itself was the outgrowth of college undergraduate "bull sessions" years in the past. The primary purpose of the participating humanitarian Harvard dreamers had been to devise a kind of aerial lighthouse for fishermen and other mariners. If an identifiable satellite could be projected into outer space, they reasoned, it would circle the earth forever. Seventeen years later, one of these visionaries, who has accumulated enough money to finance the venture, is still dedicated to the prevention of shipwrecks.

After the moonlike machine was built, it was launched prematurely by accident, carrying with it a number of the cooperating inventors and their families. A year or so later, it was spotted in the outer atmosphere—at R.A. 27° 11'; south declination 34° 49'—nine thousand miles from the earth's center and five thousand miles from the surface; it was off course, but intact. Ingham, who was able to see the thirty-seven or so persons on the satellite, learned to communicate with them by Morse code. The unpremeditated pioneer astronauts were happy, " 'Much happier,' Ingham discovered, 'than if they lived in sixth floors in Paris, in lodgings in London, or even in tenement houses in Phoenix Place, Boston' " (Works, IV, 80). The yarn is entertaining, even if heavy with the paraphernalia of pseudoastronomy, pseudosociology, and pseudologic.

The possibilities of twisting scientific and technological formulas to absurd consequences led Hale into writing a number of other stories and light essays from "The Dot and Line Alphabet" and "The Last of the Florida" that were in his earliest collection to "Susan's Escort," the title of his last. The first two are minor; but "Susan's Escort"—the most gentle and gentlemanly Frankenstein monster ever invented—is an example of Hale's undiminished humor in his best vein. In "The Lost Palace," which is dominated by satire rather than either comedy or science, Hale describes the method of getting a train across a river without a bridge or a ferry. In "Dick's Christmas," the hero, a boy genius, invented the better mousetrap— equally effective for capturing cockroaches—and later added such greater inventions as a new "jib-key and cut-off and smoke-consumer."

Several of Hale's most readable humorous stories, which are neither quasi-Utopian nor psuedoscientific, are fantastic tall tales; but they are not the rough backwoods type of Davy Crockett nor the frontier type of the younger Mark Twain: they are undiluted Brahmin yarns from Beacon Hill and the Harvard campus. Two of the best, "The Survivor's Story" and "The Skeleton in the Closet," are, contrary to their morbid titles, uninhibited fantasy. Each illustrates a narrative device favored by Hale of improvising a series of anecdotes that lead by hit or by miss to an end that is surprisingly different from the beginning. In "The Survivor's Story," a liars' contest among a group of travelers waiting for a train is rambling though lively; but in "The Skeleton in the Closet," an outrageous parody of postwar, now-it-can-be-told revelations, the preposterous anecdotes are tightly related by cause and effect. The supposed narrator, a Confederate bureaucrat, identifies the most serious shortage of the war—not coffee, not snuff—as hoops for stylish skirts, "skeletons, we used to call them." Returning to Virginia from a hush-hush confidential assignment in New York, the narrator smuggled a large supply of the latest high fashion models for the women of his household and enabled them to discard their bent, infirm, obsolete hoops. Then the havoc began—broken legs, jammed machinery, accidents and mistakes, each with its separate absurd anecdote—climaxing in "the ruin of the Confederate army, navy, ordinance, and treasury: and it led to the capture of the poor President too" (*Works*, I, 320).[13]

V *Education, Inspiration, Religion*

For convenience rather than by theory, Hale preferred to write short stories in which humor predominated. This supply-and-demand arrangement worked to his advantage professionally and was certainly satisfactory for his readers; little of his serious fiction shows the spontaneous vitality of his best told humorous incidents. In fact, his patriotic stories, even three in which his hero George Washington appears, include no worthy successor to *The Man Without a Country*, and several ventures into pseudohistory produced only one contribution to his better work. This is "The Story of Oello," an excursion into primitivism, a rare experiment for Hale. The doctrine is his familiar advocacy of usefulness, but the story is told in a mannered style that suggests that it is truly a legend of how civilization was brought to prehistoric Peru before the Spanish conquest.

"Hands Off," another story outside Hale's most familiar patterns, is a fantasy that is as philosophical as Hale ever permitted himself to become; for it is based upon a speculation: how would human history have been altered if some single event had not occurred as it did? If the youth Yussuf Ben Yacoub—"as we say, Joseph, son of Jacob"—had immediately escaped from the slave traders and had returned to his father, how would this happy reunion have affected later events? Most disastrously, the spirit narrator answered, for what appears evil to a man is God's goodness to mankind. Without Joseph, Egypt would have had no granaries, no civilization; the Mediterranean area would have been subjected by Carthage and the Molochites; neither Greece nor Rome could have prevailed against heathenism. Joseph's misfortunes were, therefore, the source of his contributions to cosmic progress. In theological terms, which Hale hesitates to use, God knows best.[14] Though Hale's excursions into church history were seldom successful, his last attempt at Biblical fiction retains interest as a document. In "If Jesus Came to Boston" (1894), which benefits from Hale's absorption in contemporary municipal conditions, even his poorly sketched incidents become more vital than his dead sketches of the past.

The themes Hale used (most) often in his prosaic educational tales are the responses of ordinary persons to circumstance and the unforeseen effects of commonplace acts of kindness. The central characters, frequently young women, undergo little soul searching, rarely feel guilty, and proceed to solve their problems through intelligence and resourcefulness without resorting to exhibitionism or trickery. "Neither Scrip Nor Money" (*Works*, III, 113–148) is one of the simpler examples in which a young woman church worker spends an entire day walking and riding around Boston helping people with services. In a more complicated version, "One Good Turn" (1893), a young woman lets a man go ahead of her to consult a doctor; but she never learns the results of her generosity: that five hundred babies' lives are saved and that a war is averted.

Though not guiltless, Hale seldom succumbed, even at his most earnest, to verbalized emotional clichés. In "Christmas in Cooney Camp" (1883), a critical corrective to flagrant sentimentalism, Hale presents a narrative that is partly a parody and an imitation, but is fundamentally an appeal to reason. The first half of his story is roughly parallel with Bret Harte's "How Santa Claus came to Simpson's Bar," (1872) but it contains enough easily recognizable allusions to "The Outcasts of Poker Flat," "The Luck of Roaring Camp," and other tales to imply a general disapproval of melodramatic sensationalism.

Hale's setting, a northern lumber camp that is as rough and ready as the California of Harte's Argonauts, needs no highwayman or pistol shots or drops of blood on the Christmas toys. He does show,

though, how the toughest lumberjack in camp sacrifices his comfort
to make a child happy: "Just as her little eyes were closing in sleep,
she murmured half to herself, 'Dod bless Santy Caus for sendin' my
dolly.' " To which Hale's supposed narrator—a college student from
Lansing, Michigan—adds a few moralizing sentences about the
mixed generosity and blindness of humanity: "I wish I could close
this story by telling how this little incident started a permanent
reform in camp. . . . [but] Jack and Bill and Tom and all the rest
went back to their old ways. They drank and swore and fought as
hard as ever. . . ." Somehow or other, he admits, everybody must
have been the better for this emotional spree, but they remained
human, sadly enough, for "our eyes are blinded."[15]

The best written of Hale's moral tales is the historical novelette *In
His Name* (1873), an extended "Christmas story" that expresses the
faith and hope of the season. Its narrative effectiveness is solidly
based upon techniques that Hale understood but often disregarded:
specifically, a balance of parts, a unified plan, and a level of expres-
siveness above journalistic expediency. The action is completed
within a period of three weeks but the crucial part is compressed
into three days. The telling, unhurried and economical, has few
misleading digressions. The picturesque geographical background
of Lyons, France, and its vicinity is clearly described. The social
conditions of the year 1192 are plausibly sketched, with sufficient
detail for a novelette whose theme is neither historical nor sociological. In keeping with the atmosphere of his story, Hale modified his
usual American diction and speech rhythms to give a foreign impression without employing exotic archaisms. He was permanently
proud of the result, and he was doubly happy because of its critical
and commercial success.

A hundred years after this novelette's publication, its fragile tale
has lost its original charm; and its technical devices have become as
unfashionable as its sentiments. The failure, relatively speaking, as
an artistic creation has two causes that are more serious than minor
flaws. One is the superficial characterization that would be considered adequate for a short story with the same theme but that is not
full enough for the longer story that Hale published. The second
defect is the lack, so common in historical novels, of plausibility.
The plot answers the limited question—will Father John be able to
save Félicie's life?—with her recovery on Christmas day; but the
major question of the conflict between individual conscience and

constituted authority—or between action and creed—is left un-
answered. The scene of reconciliation between a heretic and a cleric
in the final chapters carries no conviction. It is historically unlikely,
except as an oddity of 1192, and imaginatively impossible within the
framework of the story. The logical though inconclusive denoue-
ment would have been to save the girl's life but to continue the feud
between outlawed virtue and an intrenched, self-righteous but
somewhat uneasy establishment.[16]

CHAPTER 5

Longer Fiction: Novels and Tracts

EXCEPT for the early *Margaret Percival in America* (1850) that Hale wrote in collaboration with his sister Lucretia, his eighteen novels—a misleading term to apply to most of these stories—were published within the relatively short span of twenty-one years. They began in 1871 with Hale's first lend-a-hand story, *10 × 1 = 10 (Ten Times One is Ten)*, and ended with *Sybil Knox* (1892), the last lend-a-hand story, and *The New Harry and Lucy* (1892), also a collaboration with Lucretia Hale. The similarities and repetitions among several of them are not accidental, for they were intended to promote the same social attitudes and to appeal to readers of the same magazines, primarily Hale's own *Old and New* (1870–1875) and its successor *Lend a Hand*.

Outside the usual patterns and formulas of Hale's longer fiction are *Philip Nolan's Friends* (1877), a patriotic historical romance; *East and West* (1892), a more realistic historical novel; and *In His Name* (1873), a novelette set in twelfth century France. For different reasons *A Wolf at the Door* (1877) and *G. T. T.* (1877) avoid Hale's reformist theses, the former because it was published anonymously and the latter from sheer vacation relaxation.[1]

A dozen other titles are the labels of narratives that depict, selectively, contemporary or almost contemporary American life for the purpose of stimulating public activities for improvement. Therefore, the interest in these tracts, which are devoid of distinction in plot or characterization, is their social import, their themes, and the descriptive details designed to induce belief. Although the chronology of composition is neither esthetically nor technically important, it provides a convenient table for identifying the topics upon which Hale wrote.[2]

57

I   Margaret Percival in America *(1850)*

Hale's first extended narrative was a Massachusetts Unitarian reply to British High Church Anglicanism. Hale wrote it with his sister Lucretia as a sequel to the original *Margaret Percival,* the work of Elizabeth Missing Sewell, a more experienced novelist, and her brother William, a prominent English churchman. The Hale performance, though a limping and verbose apprentice work, is a clear statement of convictions that he never abandoned. In the original English story, Margaret, a sensitive young girl, had been tempted by Catholicism—like John Henry Newman and other Anglicans of the 1840s—but had been persuaded by her uncle, a British bulldog type of ecclesiastic, to retain her original faith as the only true one. Hale and his sister objected both to this intolerant exclusiveness and to the bullying tactics by which the girl's quest for spiritual truth had been, as they thought, prematurely terminated.

To give Margaret a second chance, they imagined her emigrating to America, befriended by a wise New England businessman, settled in a small Massachusetts town, put to work as a school teacher, surrounded by right thinking but unpolemical Unitarians, and enabled to blossom anew in this wholesome religious and political environment. The outcome is that, while retaining her faith and creed, she appreciates the integrity of other faiths and creeds as well; for she realizes that the unity of Christianity does not depend upon an absolute uniformity of theological doctrines or of church organization. She has changed, indeed, from a worried self-centered sectarian to a happy worker in the Lord's service.

Two of the agents of this transformation are a young woman, Anna Wilkie, the daughter of Margaret's first American benefactor, and a young man, Arthur Newstead. Anna is the ideal, if not of all Bostonian Unitarians, at least of Edward Everett Hale. She has a "passion" for Fénelon, and she enjoys reading "the most beautiful of Martineau's sermons"(9). She quotes lines of verse by John Keble and Elizabeth Barrett which she has memorized. She has copied into her commonplace book passages from the philosopher Blaise Pascal and the churchman Jeremy Taylor which she reads at length to a sickly friend. She likes John Ruskin too—"the true, beautiful descriptions of our friend of the Modern Painters"(53)—and approves of Charlotte Bronte's *Jane Eyre* because of its optimistic conclusion. She has studied music theory enough to be thrilled by the "great poems" of Ludwig von Beethoven and Felix Mendelssohn; knows Latin well enough to read Virgil and German well enough to translate Goethe's technical scientific *Metamorphosis of Plants;* and she owns a copy of Ralph Waldo Emerson's *Essays* in which she keeps specimens of pressed flowers. She is a walking and talking encyclopedia.

Arthur Newstead, another indefatigable conversationalist, is a young man, possibly very young, who is introduced as a cynical Byronist—"a hater of his species," as Anna banteringly chides him (35). Far from a Byronic misanthrope, young Newstead later shows himself an enthusiastic *come-outer*, which, in the vocabulary of his time, is a radical reformer who would be called *activist* today. An idealistic youth, he has the wild ambition of restoring Palestine economically as the "centre of the world's action"(138).

A third contribution to Margaret Percival's education in tolerance was the democratic Massachusetts society into which she had been transplanted. British customs and institutions no longer fitted the land or the people; the Established Church was no longer the natural church of a new society. In one discussion of this subject (ch. 25, 161–78), incidental references to Americanisms in speech, such as the Yankee pronunciation *du tell*, lead to a conception of the United States as the melting pot of races, which in turn leads to the ideal of religious pluralism.

Although *Margaret Percival in America* is dull fiction, weak in narrative appeal, it contained the substance of persuasive tracts, many of which Hale himself was to write later.

II *Lend-a-Hand Novels*

In keeping with Hale's deepened commitment to social action, his first serial for his magazine *Old and New* announced his most ambitious theme. Though a fantasy, *10 × 1 = 10* has a purpose as serious as one can be; that is, in the original subtitle, *The Possible Reformation* or, more properly, the re-formation of society. The book is a nest of anecdotes held together intellectually by a mathematical formula and, as narrative, by a framework in which the Reverend Colonel Frederic Ingham chats with his fellow volunteers in the service of Giuseppe Garibaldi, the liberator of Italy. The story that Ingham tells his companions begins in a New England railway station where ten mourners, previously unacquainted, find that the only train is five hours late; it ends, twenty-seven years later, around 1882 (some twelve years after the date of publication), with the re-formation of the world. The theme is the application of Christian power—the ultimate virtues of faith, hope, and love—to regenerate society.

Harry Wadsworth, the dead station agent, had been a truly Christian character (Hale does not use the term Christlike); and the ten mourners at his funeral were like disciples since each had owed some kind of spiritual awakening to him. One was a humble servant woman whose son had been rescued from a life of crime; another was a gold miner whose life had been saved when Harry Wadsworth dispersed a gang of ruffians intent upon murder. Each mourner had resolved, independently, to live in the spirit of Harry Wadsworth; and their efforts, initiating an irresistible chain reaction, were successful. "Nine triads of years were enough each to add a zero to the figure which stood for that one man. Ten times one was ten, 10 times 1 = 10. There was one zero. But as nine zeros were added, in twenty-seven years the 1 became 1,000,000,000—ONE THOUSAND MILLION. This proved to be the number of the Happy World!"(148). This fortunate outcome was hope unrealized, not prophecy; yet Hale, who was never a sour reformer, could look about in 1898 without bitterness that so little improvement had been made and with satisfaction that so much was in the process of being accomplished.

The gospel, if it might be called that, had been spread through voluntary Harry Wadsworth clubs or congregations: singing societies, baseball teams, sewing schools, and formally organized clubs. "All you could say of these thousand people was that, in six years, the life of that young railroad freight-agent had quickened their lives, had made them less selfish, and less worldly"(78). The total creed was expressed in four mottoes, the first three equivalent to faith, hope, and love, respectively, and the fourth a combination of three into a rule for action: "to look up and not down; to look forward and not back; to look out and not in; and to lend a hand"(130).

Hale's satisfaction in the success of *Ten Times One Is Ten* was justified.[3] Not as an art work, but as a parable, the story was surprisingly fruitful. Hale's call to service was immediately commended by thoughtful idealists like Helen Hunt Jackson, and clubs based on the mottoes were formed by "unselfish people, who met, not for 'mutual improvement' but with some definite plans for other people." Hale wrote an account of these clubs for the preface of the slightly revised version which was reprinted in the third volume of his *Works*. Such clubs adopted a variety of names—"Harry Wadsworth Helpers," the "Look-Up Legion" (which extended through five hundred Sunday Schools), the "Welcome and Correspondence Club"—and from some of these groups the King's Daughters and the Epworth League were formed. The magazine *Lend a Hand*, established in 1886, lasted for several years under that name; and a number of charitable enterprises were sponsored at home and abroad. Although the ideals of Harry Wadsworth did not sweep the world, notwithstanding the irrefutable mathematical formula by which one swelled to a thousand million, Hale's story and its sequels worked in the direction of goodwill and good deeds.

Except in short fiction like "Stand and Wait" (1870), in which the Order of Loving Service is prominent, Hale's next fictional blueprint for social regeneration was *Our New Crusade* (1875); and it contained fifty thousand words of directions for saving a local option town for temperance. The book itself is far from exciting, in spite of a runaway horse, a dangerous fire, and a college fraternity convention. It offers no rivalry to T. S. Arthur's masterpiece *Ten Nights in a Bar-Room*. Its program attracted less immediate attention in the mass communications media than the direct action exploits of Carry Nation, and it had less lasting attention than the uncompromising proposal of Hale's friend Frances E. Willard. Although the book exhibits undisputed practical sense about curbing alcoholism by substituting service clubs for saloons, it is a pedestrian literary performance, less imaginative than *Ten Times One Is Ten*.

Mrs. Merriam's Scholars (1878), another direct continuation of *10 × 1 = 10*, is better fiction by any standard than *Our New Crusade*. As an attempt to combine Hale's two purposes of improving society and of devising a narrative to carry the message implicitly, this novel is not completely successful; but it is distinguished among his *invented examples*, as he called them, for the dominance of the narrative over the exhortation. Moreover, it is, in the main, a factual account of an aspect of the Civil War that had been neglected in the major historical novels of events from 1864 and 1865. Hale's subject is a young girl's experiences in Washington, D.C., and Virginia as a volunteer teacher for the Sanitary Commission in "levelling up" Negro children.

Subsequent additions to the lend-a hand series were less successful. One of these is a small book called *Four and Five* (1891) in which four boys, the eldest approaching twenty, engage in such good works as replacing a washed-out bridge for a country blacksmith, installing an irrigation system on an old woman's farm, and establishing a boys' club for singing, Bible reading, and sports. The failure of *Sybil Knox* (1892) is more to be regretted; for Hale had put greater than customary effort into it by devising plots and subplots along with his messages and admonitions and by introducing characters and settings outside his usual range of effects. Since these mixed elements failed to combine, the result is a sad example of artistic chaos.

The story, which opens well, shows Sybil Knox as an intelligent and attractive young widow from Vermont who has been abroad for ten years, the last seven in the American colony in Rome. Her return and the stages of her readmission to American society would have justified Hale's complete title, *Sybil Knox, or, Home Again, a Story of To-day*. After the urbane opening, the theme shifts without warning from a question of comparative national cultures to the pettiness of harmless gossip. Attention is drawn to a group of lady reformers of the "Send Me" order, a subsidiary of the Lend-a-Hand Society. Even the constitution of this organization is entered on the record—fortunately, it is short—with directions for establishing branches. After this interruption, the story of Sybil's return to Vermont diverges permanently into a protracted account of detective work by her future husband, courtroom scenes in Tennessee, and an attack on financial piracy. Too many good causes, supported with justifiable righteous indignation, have superseded a potentially rewarding novel of character.[4]

III   *Everyday People*

Outside the series of Ten-Times-One stories, but not far removed, Hale wrote numerous books to illustrate and promote good works. Some were as short as the ninety-eight tiny pages of *Back to Back*, but they fit no set schedule of publication and follow no definite line of development in theme or construction. Designed for casual reading, they have little claim to careful attention except as commentary on the national scene.[5]

Ups and Downs: An Every-Day Novel (1873), one of Hale's more successful works of this kind, is substantial—ninety thousand words or more—and begins deceptively, as if it might justify its subtitle and be more of a story than a tract. The opening scene shows the Harvard campus during commencement about 1840. Jasper Rising, although an orphan, is the most popular graduate of the year, the man most likely to succeed, and the star orator of the ceremonies. At the day's end, he receives a fateful letter from his uncle's home in the Michigan backwoods. The lumber mill has burned, the uncle has died, and the fortune has been entirely swept away. Jasper read the letter twice, lighted a cigar, and blew smoke rings. "What does all this mean?" a classmate asked. "It means, my dear boy, that I am a beggar"—and his present circumstances contrast with the professor of divinity's prediction of the afternoon: "I remember no young man who has so auspicious a beginning"(22).

After leaving Harvard with his top-notch education, "the best our country can afford"(2), Jasper began his real education, one different yet complementary, that led him to modest professional success and absolute happiness. His moral integrity—not dependent upon church membership—is manifested in the only incident of political significance in the book: his refusal to accept a government contract for two hundred wagons for the army during the Mexican war. " 'I do not believe in the administration, and I do not believe in the war'," he told a colonel from the Engineers. " 'I do not choose to make money out of what I think a public wrong' "(100).

Less serious in purpose than *Ups and Downs*, the briefer narrative of *G. T. T.* is even closer to the possible experience of the original readers. When Hale wrote this book in 1877 for the Town and Country Series, the initials no longer meant what they had thirty years before, a loss of meaning that gave him the opportunity for a preface in which he revealed that they stood for "Gone to Texas." Hale's book, a byproduct of his preparation for his historical novel *Philip Nolan's Friends*, was also the result of another fascination, one duly advertised in the subtitle *The Adventures of a Pullman*. Thus it is a travel novel of sorts, or at least a romance of transportation, a happy book in the mood of a carefree vacation.

As a novel, *G. T. T.* is pointless; it is a double romance between persons admirably suited to each other socially and morally but lifeless as fictional characters. As a travelogue, it is a continuous stream of observation and comment, mostly light chatter, about a dozen subjects. In a moderate extension of the usual objects of his attention, Hale introduced the words, and sometimes the music, of songs as different as the old favorite "Blue Juniata"; an excerpt from

Rigoletto; Norwegian, Spanish, French, and German airs—appropriate to his theme of the merging of races in the progress of America; and two Negro spirituals, although they struck him as *weird,* "Nobody knows the trouble I've had" and "I sought my Lord in de wilderness."[6]

In contrast to the light localized satire on Bostonians in the anonymous *The Wolf at the Door* (1877), the story called *The Fortunes of Rachel* (1884) is one of Hale's most earnest surveys of American life. As a statement of conditions, problems, and ideals, it ranks among his most successful books. A Cinderella type story, it is too good to be true—for both Rachel and the United States—but not too good to be desired.

Rachel Finley herself is more fortunate than Cinderella, for she has many godmothers and no vicious sisters. Coming to America in 1879, she arrives as an adolescent orphan waif; a penniless foreigner, her fortunes take her, after a swift passage through Boston social service agencies, to longer residence in a New Hampshire village, in bustling Chicago, in the Rockies, and in the national capital. When her husband, a trust-busting attorney, is appointed to the Supreme Court, all ends well. As befits a fairy tale, the last incidents of Hale's story, including the election of a reform administration, are projected into the future (since his book was published in 1884), the first year of the twentieth century. The mining town riots, the financial "crash of 1893"(206), and the economic liberation of the people were all products of Hale's imagination.

With his voracious appetite for new books and new solutions, Hale read many of the political and economic novels in vogue during the decade of the 1880s.[7] No evidence suggests, however, that Hale's novels of 1888 were directly influenced by them; and publication of three books, recently but not simultaneously written, within the year was the publishers' choice, not a new campaign by Hale. *My Friend the Boss; A Story of To-Day* is several stories, each commonplace in itself but agreeably combined into a tract—what Hale was accustomed to call a parable—both lively and perspicacious. The boss himself, a prosperous local businessman, is the leading right-thinking citizen of a Midwestern city, the only kind of *boss* whom Hale approved.

The liveliest parts of Hale's book are convincing descriptions of several civic meetings: a temperance lecture at which the speaker is pelted with vegetables and rotten eggs; a gathering of athletes, "very muscular Christians, with their pretty wives and daughters"(22); and a convention of ministers advocating, more or less, interdenominational cooperation. Better reading than these is an hilarious description of laying the cornerstone of a local academy of fine arts (ch. XIII, 71–84), the exact image of provincial bumpkins of the United States, vintage of 1888 or any subsequent year.

With *Mr. Tangier's Vacations* (1888), Hale returned to his familiar East Coast locations, to his standard theme of improving village life, and to his usual slight narrative burdened by incongruous references and parenthetical comments. Curious in a book so lacking design is Hale's obvious fondness of fiction artistically planned, for he refers approvingly to Howells, Jane Austen, and Hawthorne. Most indicative of his awareness of esthetic form are passages from the second part of his story:

The reader has seen with his [Mr. Tangier's, a metropolitan lawyer] eyes thus far, and has gone only where he has gone. . . . From this point, for several chapters, this little story of a little town might be told in four different ways, according as the incidents which concern our readers were told from Mr. Tangier's point of view, from Miss Bessy Curtry's [a village schoolmistress], from Mr. Drummond's [a fisherman], or from Miss Remington's [a cultured affluent philanthropist]. Most stories may be told in many ways, as Mr. Browning's poem of *The Ring and the Book* has proved so well.(192)

In the next chapter, Robert Browning's method—or is it Henry James'?—is formally announced: "And now the reader must follow our story for a little from the schoolmistress's point of view"(204). To conclude the narrative, Hale devises two parallel, simultaneous conversations by pairs of lovers. Each couple is in a separate carriage and is driven from the railway station to the town meeting-house in which the joy of reunion accompanies the removal of misunderstandings. Thus the novel ends in a double romance, the formula that Hale had mocked midway:

. . . she [Miss Tunstall, one of the vacationers] kept a subscription for the summer at Harper's and at the Seaside Library, and so received, almost every day, two new novels. Most of them were wretched, as need hardly be said. For even the brave nineteenth century, with all its correlation of forces, has devised no machinery which shall produce more than ten good novels in a year. So that four thousand and nine hundred and ninety of the year's manufacture must be bad, most of them very bad. But for all this the "Boarders," as Mrs. Fairbanks [the landlady] called them, cared but little. So that there were two heroes, two heroines, a difficulty in the middle, and two weddings at the end, they were satisfied.(217–18)

Hale is laughing at himself; he is giving the shallow boarders and their like exactly what they expect, but he is adding the message of lending a hand, doing "something tangible and visible"(105).

Hale's third long story published in 1888, *How They Lived in Hampton*, is completely a piece; it is pointed straight at a goal, it fulfills no definition of a *novel*, and it is a unique work that only Hale would have written. When he reprinted it in his selected *Works* in 1900, he was reaffirming his confidence in industrial cooperatives and was evincing his satisfaction about the skill with which he had expounded his thesis. The plan had appealed to him years before 1888, and he had outlined the operation of a cooperative mill so authoritatively that he had been offered the management of several.

His first fictional version of *How They Lived in Hampton* reached the public in 1877 in "Back to Back," a two part story in *Harper's Magazine* (LV [November 1877], 873–84; LXVI [December 1877], 34–42), which was republished a year later as Number 48 of Harper's Half-Hour Series of short books. It remains a sufficiently plausible account of running a small cooperative business a century ago. Using a military analogy, Hale keeps repeating that three partners are necessary for success: two can be surrounded by enemies, but three can beat them off. The three of his story were a capitalist, a foreman in charge of rather than representing the workmen, and a manager.

Essentially the same proposal is embodied in *How They Lived in Hampton*, a much longer book with the greater scope that is in keeping with its significant subtitle, *A Study in Practical Christianity*. The economic techniques, neither Utopian nor fantastic, are an adaptation of George Holyoke's successful British cooperative enterprise, the Rockdale Plan, to American conditions in the 1880s. Not equating profit sharing with total well-being, Hale was as concerned with the social life of Hampton as with its economic success; and, as a result, he included chapters on education, religion, and other community needs. In his preface to the 1900 edition, he reasserted his faith in cooperative industry but expressed reservations about the joys of living in Hampton. "First, and chiefly, the inhabitants of such a village," he reflected, "with no other occupations than those here suggested, would become terribly sick of each other and of life" (*Works*, IX, 219). This criticism is frequently made of other imagined communities, but it is seldom admitted so frankly by those who have contrived them.

IV Last Novels

Unlike *Sybil Knox* (1892), in which disorganization bordered on the pathological, Hale's other fiction published in 1892 consists of two of his best planned productions. *East and West* (1892) is an historical novel of America at the end of the eighteenth century, and *The New Harry and Lucy* (1892) is a chatty excursion through Boston toward the end of the nineteenth. Although neither novel had the wide appeal that their ingredients warranted, they are both attractive pieces of work. *East and West* has qualities meriting at least passing mention in surveys of historical and regional fiction; and *The New Harry and Lucy*, an entertaining combination of inconsequential incidents and lively comments, is a memorial to Boston culture that is worthy of remembrance.

Like other books by Hale, *East and West* has more than one title. In England, it was published as *The New Ohio*; and its complete American title was *East and West: A Story of New-born Ohio*. Either title is appropriate, for the West is Ohio, the East is Massachusetts, and the date of the story is 1790. The theme is the lure of the frontier—what Hale called the "passion for emigration"(146) from east to west which was "the burning question of the day"(79) in and around Salem. "Serious people, who wished the prosperity of Massachusetts under its new constitution, looked most sourly on this new passion of its young people to go out of it"(70). Yet go they did, in spite of advice, reasoning, protest, and caricature; and they confronted the hardships and dangers of the wilderness for simple or complicated motives. The three young people of Hale's story leave Salem for different reasons, travel by different routes, and are reunited at a besieged cabin in the midst of an Indian uprising.

The first of these is Sarah Parris, age twenty, the belle of the Salem Valentine Day's ball. The second is her sweetheart, Harry Curwen, the spoiled darling of the community; a hero's son, he is badly in need of self-discipline and maturation. The third, Silas Ransom (the same child of the people who had enlivened *Philip Nolan's Friends*), is nominally a "retainer" but is more basically a

Yankee and the liveliest personality of the three. Sarah went west to prove her independence and to improve her character (an impossibility, since she was already perfect); Harry, to establish his manliness; Silas, because he was a Yankee.

With these characters and this itinerary, Hale easily introduced varied action and glimpses of American life on different levels: a modest party for the socially acceptable youth of Salem; a government reception in New York, with George Washington in attendance; travel down the Ohio River in the *Perseverance*, "the first steamboat which ever plied regularly in America"(125), and a Dunkard baptism at the Ephrata colony. For information about life in 1790, Hale presents New York theatrical offerings, the street brawls of Boston hoodlum gangs, the coinage, the expectations of foreign travelers in the new nation; and these topics are noted, casually or with deliberation, without regard for fast-moving action. Always the educator, Hale even pauses to define words like *flip* (a mild alcoholic beverage) and *sawyer* (a nautical term) as well as to suggest a definition of a democracy: "where every man bears his own burdens and his brother's"(118) or, in Silas Ransom's more picturesque advice to a servile European: "Take care yer don't take any of yer darned airs here. . . . You'll get yer eyes knocked out 'fore yer know it, an' good enough fer yer too"(135).

Never outgrowing his boyhood prejudice, Hale pictured the Indians of eighteenth century Ohio as, at their best, dirty, stupid, and mistreated; at their worst, more often, they were cruel and bloodthirsty.[8] The white Americans, to their shame, were not always much better. The soldiers sent to help Harry Curwen reminded him of Falstaff's regiment, and the recruiting officer must have been "an agent for the Society of Discharged Convicts"(167). Hale was not totally blinded by his patriotic fervor, which was as genuine as his faith in God but not infinite.

Of altogether different appeal is *The New Harry and Lucy*, a newspaper serial which Edward Everett Hale and his sister Lucretia wrote for the Boston *Commonwealth*. The subtitle is apt, *A Story of Boston in the Summer of 1891*; and the preface is accurate in its statement, "This is the Boston of today." In evident enjoyment of their assignment as roving reporters, the writers responded with a zest that is a tribute to both of them; for Hale was nearing seventy, and his sister was older. The sketches—newspaper columns, they would be called today—made an amusing book of three hundred pages; but the appeal is considerably greater as a document than as fiction.

The form deliberately adopted for *The New Harry and Lucy* is the old-fashioned epistolatory narrative; and the letters, which are written alternately by Mr. Harry Merton and Miss Lucy Stanford (but not to each other), record their first impressions of Boston during the summer, that time of year when nobody is in town except the people.[9] Young transplanted Vermonters, they meet in June and marry in December. Admirable young people, they are devoted to public service and are infinitely absorbant of culture. What they see is more important in the book than what they are or what they do.

The city and its suburbs abounded in wonderful admission-free museums, gardens, galleries, and libraries which Harry and Lucy wrote about enthusiastically. For special occasions, there were the Harvard class day celebration and the Harvard-Yale crew race, Boston Pops concerts, the Old South lectures, readings by Sir Edwin Arnold, and an exhibition of food products. There were theatrical performances of *Love's Labour's Lost* with Ada Rehan; *The Old Homestead; The Country Fair* with Neil Burgess (a celebrated female impersonator); and a gaudy outdoor spectacle of *The Last Days of Pompeii*—all of which received more than casual comment. Tommaso Salvini and Helena Modjeska were also acting in the city, although neither Harry nor Lucy saw them. More in their line was a temperance convention where Frances E. Willard presided and where Lady Somerset headed the foreign delegations.

The intellectual climax of the book is reached in Harry's report of a meeting of social reformers that he attended late in the year. As an old man told him, the audience consisted of "Jerusalem-cats"; and their fervor "was quite like one of the old-fashioned antislavery audiences of fifty years ago"(301). The subject was "Literature and Reform," and Colonel Higginson spoke first, in praise of Theodore Parker, Henry George, and Edward Bellamy. "Then Dr. Hale spoke," pointing out that "the people who were connected with organized institutions and wanted to have the carriage still run in the old ruts were not apt to be the people who make the proclamations of improvement"(303). As an exception, Dr. Hale eulogized William Dean Howells, an exquisite writer who also wanted to make a better world.

Such literary references were one of Hale's characteristic educational devices, for the readers of his book were being educated no less than Harry and Lucy themselves. Therefore it is no surprise to find mention, among others, of Rollo and Robinson Crusoe, Nathaniel P. Willis, and Elizabeth Stuart Phelps, and to read more formal tributes to Emerson, Lowell (who died during the year), and Howells. As humor, another of Hale's characteristic educational devices, there are such details as the longest word in Eliot's Indian Bible—Wutappesittukgussunnookwehtunkquoh—with the question of how would an American boy like to find this word in his spelling book.

CHAPTER 6

History and Journalism

I *Principles and Practices*

HALE'S historical writings, a minor part of his work, exhibit him as a talented amateur whose boyhood love of reading history inspired his ambition to write it also. Long entries in his journal during the crucial week of October 31 to November 5, 1838, show his excitement over the prospect of assisting William Hickling Prescott and his dejection over missing the appointment *(Life and Letters*, I, 53–58). Although Hale never forgot his disappointment at sixteen or relinquished the dream of becoming an important historian, editing and writing on call or by schedule appear to have been more appropriate activities for him than research in depth. Instead of a scholarly professional, he became two occasional historians: at times, he was a careful compiler and arranger of documents; at other times—much as he protested and resented the charge—he was merely a hasty popularizer.

Though himself a delighted reader of historical fiction, Hale definitely disapproved of any distortion of the facts of allegedly accurate history; yet, as befitted a journalist, he also asked that reading be made no more difficult than the content or the subject required: "For one, I am much obliged to anybody who tried to make it easy for me to read. According to me, you might as well write with white ink on white paper as write anything in a language so dull that nobody wants to read it."[1]

Dangerously unscholarly or not, Hale's ambition to be readable was a less important cause of his inferior historical writings than his unacknowledged, extraneous use of history to promote ethical purposes. Written history as he practiced it fell into two classes distinguished by their aims: to report events fully with factual accuracy or selectively to stimulate heroism. In either style his gifts of neat

71

phrasing and smooth narration seldom deserted him, but his range of sympathy and understanding was restricted by his blindness to the pathos or tragedy of history. Biography was particularly attractive to him, but his reticence about the private lives of his subjects allowed only a partial view, and his inveterate optimism produced rosy-colored pictures that strain belief.

He was tempted too often into writing or editing short biographies of persons about whom he knew or cared less than even a perfunctory sketch demands. The result was the sponsorship of such an undistinguished book as *Lights of Two Centuries* (1887) "edited by Edward Everett Hale," which included artists like Jean Antoine Watteau and Joshua Reynolds, composers like Georg Friedrich Händel and Joseph Haydn, poets like Robert Burns and Friedrich von Schiller, such favorites of his as Robert Fulton and Eli Whitney, and personal friends like Emerson and Longfellow. Though it is doubtful that Hale wrote these pedestrian sketches, he evidently supplied the footnotes from "original" or standard sources, and he sponsored a number of similar collections—biographies of *Master Spirits*, single volume "libraries" of history, sets of books for "young folks," and portraits and principles of great men for the subscription trade. Some of these publications were unworthy of his talent, however well intended they were as popular education.[2]

The unequal value of Hale's short biographical and historical articles was due to several such causes which can be verified by examples. In 1894, he wrote sketches of Nathan Hale and Goethe for a subscription set *Great Men and Famous Women*, published by Selman Hess, in which he was joined by a miscellany of name writers as diverse as Henry George and Theodore Roosevelt, Ignatius Donnelly and H. Rider Haggard, Will Carleton and Ella Wheeler Wilcox. Hale was obviously well equipped by fact and temperament to write about the Revolutionary hero, but he was poorly qualified to discuss Goethe.

Unlike such ventures, however prompted, the chapters which Hale contributed to his friend Justin Winsor's *Narrative and Critical History of America* (1884–1889), the most distinguished cooperative work of its time, are typical of his best historical writing.[3] Of similar quality were his thoroughly researched contributions to Winsor's monumental *Memorial History of Boston* (1880–1881).

Among Hale's historical essays, his introduction to a new edition of *General Sir William Howe's Orderly Book* (1890) is admirably systematic and informative.[4] Like an academic researcher Hale provides a history of the manuscript, references to previous limited use by Jared Sparks and George Bancroft, and an indication of its value in relating "every detail of the administration and discipline of the English Army in the siege of Boston" (iii). A genealogy of the Howe family follows and a summary of the broader military events of the years that the *Orderly Book* covers. An objective description of other documents reprinted with the *Orderly Book* completes the introduction in accordance with the best professional practices of the time.

With less display of technical scholarship, Hale prepared a stimulating, elementary *History of the United States* through the War of 1812 for the Chautauqua Reading Circles (1887). It is a straightforward story that has been frequently told, sometimes more discerningly but never more sincerely. Nevertheless, the best part of this *History of the United States* is the preface in which Hale explains his purposes and ideals. He invites his readers to refer to fuller accounts and, more significantly, urges them to become historians themselves, "to undertake the preservation of the materials of local history in the neighborhoods in which they live"(8). His counsel on this point remains sound: "There can scarcely be named a part of the United States—perhaps there cannot be named a part of the United States—where careful conversation with the aged, careful exploration of the public records, and careful investigation of files of old letters, or of old books of account, would not bring to light much which would have historic value"(8). Hale's entire preface is such a usable, brief guide to materials and methods of research that only tape recorders and computers are needed to bring it up to date.

II *American Heroes*

Hale's major individual heroes were George Washington, Benjamin Franklin, and an honorary American, Christopher Columbus. For allusion and reference they served him well, as did the two institutions he admired most—the Colonial America from Columbus to the beginning of Thomas Jefferson's administration, and Massachusetts from Plymouth Rock to eternity. As a result of Hale's interests, his most substantial historical writing was a compilation in two bulky volumes, *Franklin in France* (1887–88), on which his son Edward Everett Hale, Jr., who was then in his early twenties, helped as assistant or collaborator. It is a collection of letters and

other documents, few of which had been previously published, with
annotations and narrative links by the editors. With its emphasis on
Franklin's public services, the material was necessarily selective,
but Hale's primary aim was fidelity to fact: "It is one of the felicities
of studying history a century after the events described, that, with
the facilities given in the opening of archives, we are able to see
both sides of the shield, and to understand the embroidery better,
because we can look at the unfaded colors on the reverse"(II, 417).

Hale's book disappointed some readers because of its failure to
justify its title fully. In spite of its omission of a disclosure of
Franklin's lively personal life, the work was recognized as a contribution to knowledge of diplomatic history and of the life of
Franklin. It offered new material for study and it was accepted for
half a century by scholars as an authoritative work on the subject.[5]
Though little of the published criticism then or later duplicated the
effusiveness of George Bancroft's eulogy of "your delicious book on
Franklin," the historian was correct in his praise of the book as
"exceedingly pleasant to read." Hale himself might have mentioned
without undue self-praise that the extremely valuable collection of
Frankliniana in his book had been secured by and for the Library of
Congress through his recommendation and only after he had appeared before a puzzled congressional committee to testify to and
explain the value of this material.[6]

Hale's biography of Washington (1888), a relatively unimportant
book, was an admirably balanced appraisal in its day; it was barely
critical, never iconoclastic, but far from sentimental idolatry. Although circulated by its publishers, G. P. Putnam's Sons, in their
series "The Boys' and Girls' Library of American Biography," it
more clearly strikes the level of "family reading," and it fully justified Hale's own title, *The Life of George Washington Studied
Anew.* His new material was Washington's voluminous diaries,
which he paraphrased skillfully and from which he quoted extensively. *The Life of Christopher Columbus* (1891), following the same
plan, was superficial.

The Story of Massachusetts (1891), another of Hale's failures, is
less trustworthy than the modest and frankly juvenile guidebook,
Historic Boston and its Neighborhood (1898) that was published in a
series of "home reading books" under the editorship of William T.
Harris, the United States Commissioner of Education. The subject
was congenial in itself, and Hale was permitted to arrange his mate-

rial within a narrative framework, as described in the book's subtitle: "An historical pilgrimage personally conducted by Edward Everett Hale, arranged for seven days." The narrative itself, which concerns the visit to Boston of Mrs. Frederic Ingham and her children, is not obtrusive enough to become bothersome; and the illustrations, while totally without artistic merit, are interestingly varied, ranging beyond monuments and churches to cultural subjects such as the Harvard library, current street scenes, a facsimile of William Bradford's manuscript of the Mayflower Compact, and, as frontispiece, "The Hub of the Universe" itself.

Hale's text is graceful in expression, with hardly more apparent organization than casual conversation. A chapter like "Bunker Hill" or "Harvard College" is not exclusively about the announced subject. Happy literary allusions are scattered throughout: a ballad that Longfellow wrote at Hale's suggestion;[7] commendation of Cooper's *Lionel Lincoln* and Mrs. Stowe's *Oldtown Folks;* tributes to bookstores, present and past; and a section on Boston street names in which Hale states that Berkeley Street was named for the philosopher and "Clarendon was named for the Clarendon Press in Oxford"(157).[8]

Equally successful on a yet smaller scale was Hale's Boston Municipal Oration for 1897 (reprinted in *Works,* Volume VIII). It was an impressive occasion, for Hale's predecessors in this annual event included John Hancock for 1774, John Quincy Adams for 1793, Horace Mann for 1842, Oliver Wendell Holmes for 1863, and others of almost equal eminence. At the age of seventy-five, Hale looked like a prophet and, according to reports, sounded like one. He spoke on "The Contribution of Boston to American Independence" with such conviction and such self-identification that he seemed, at least to younger listeners, like a participant in the events he described.

III   *What the Magazines Wanted*

Dr. Hale's pride in his accomplishments as a working newspaperman and as a magazine editor is obvious in numerous casual references and in the autobiographical sketches "Editorial Duty" and "Literary and Editorial Work" published in his collected *Works* in Volume X and Volume VI respectively. When he recalled with gratitude his early journalistic experiences, he credited them for training him in clear expression and in the habit of rapid writing.

These early experiences, which he never recounted completely, began with childhood games imitating his father's paper, the *Advertiser*, and advanced to genuine news assignments for the newspaper while he was still a college undergraduate. His connection with the *Advertiser* did not cease after its sale in 1865.[9] His first work on a magazine, assisting his brother with the *Boston Miscellany* in 1842, provided some of his happiest memories. Shortly afterward, he edited as a young preacher the *Sunday School Gazette* in Worcester. Considerably later, beginning in 1857, he was an associate of Frederic H. Hedge on the board of the *Christian Examiner*, the leading Unitarian journal. During the Civil War, he was assistant editor of the *Army and Navy Journal* (1863–1864), writing unsigned articles for it, and for a large number of newspapers in addition to the *Advertiser*. These and other temporary activities were preliminary to founding in 1870 his own magazine, *Old and New*. As partner in publishing firms, he also understood the book trade in all its stages between soliciting manuscripts, printing and selling them, and protecting international copyrights.

His favorite journalistic outlets were magazines, for which he supplied articles on request for nearly seventy years. In 1840 he entered this field near the top, in one of the most respected general circulation periodicals in the nation, the already venerable *North American Review*, founded in 1815. When the equally eminent *Atlantic Monthly* was established in 1857, he became a contributor in the magazine's second year. He was still contributing, infrequently, to both until the mid-1890s. Of even longer duration was his connection with the *Proceedings of the American Antiquarian Society of Worcester* for which he wrote frequent notes and scholarly articles from as early as 1849 to 1907.

In all probability, the full extent of Hale's signed contributions to magazines is unknowable. Among the better known or long-lived publications are listed *Harper's*, *Scribner's*, the *Independent*, *Review of Reviews*, the *Century*, *Cosmopolitan*, *McClure's*, the *National Geographic*. His work also appeared in such once popular magazines as *Sartain's*, *Galaxy*, *Frank Leslie's*, the New York *Ledger*, the *Hearth and Home*, the *Christian Union*, and *Our Young Folks*. The titles of other periodicals suggest in themselves the wide scope of his interests: from the *Chautauquan* to the *Harvard Graduates' Magazine*; from the Massachusetts Historical Society *Proceedings* and the *Magazine of American History* to the *Critic*,

Current Literature, the *Writer;* from the *Monthly Religious Magazine, Sunday Afternoon,* the *American Journal of Theology* and other religious journals to *Education,* the *Charities Review,* the *Nationalist, Forum,* and other exponents of public welfare and reform.

Hale's connection with the *North American Review* began as a youthful book reviewer,[10] a notoriously difficult assignment in which he made the easy mistakes of excessive censure on the one hand and of excessive praise on the other. The latter is the less objectionable, for it does no harm to predict long life for unimportant fiction like *Cecil, a Peer,* though obviously the lengthy extracts do not justify the reviewer's enthusiasm.[11] Violent attack, however, is a moral lapse that is totally uncharacteristic of Hale in maturity and that is explicable only as intoxication with the power of the anonymous poison pen.

The victim of Hale's ferocity was Charles Anthon, the already famous professor of Classical languages at Columbia University, whom Hale accused of plagiarism, arrogance, and ignorance of Greek.[12] At the time, July 1840, Hale was considerably short of twenty years of age; and his accomplishments as a Classicist were restricted to graduation from Harvard as a bachelor of arts and to a year's work as instructor in the Boston Latin School. Anthon's book was a "new edition" of a textbook, *The Greek Reader,* published in New York; and Hale observed in it suspicious parallels with another textbook published in Boston in 1832.

Hale's anonymous attack drew rejoinders, including an eleven page pamphlet from the *Knickerbocker Magazine,* published in New York. Hale continued the debate, which was extended to three parts, with the conclusion, at least to Hale's satisfaction, that Anthon or his unnamed assistants must have borrowed from the Boston edition with which Edward Everett appears to have had some connection. The textbook no doubt eventually disappeared from use, but Charles Anthon's reputation has somehow survived Hale's attack.

Even as an anonymous reviewer Hale soon learned how to direct his indignation with better aim and how to control his tongue. In a review of Tom Taylor's life of Benjamin Robert Haydon, he wrote favorably of the book, much as he disliked Haydon as artist and man.

Other reviews of this decade gave Hale the opportunity to sharpen his wit on a wide variety of subjects.[13] He provided descriptive notes as needed on antiquarian documents and books on education, and he wrote common sense appraisals of poems and novels. He enjoyed Alfred Tennyson's *Maud*, was enthusiastic about Longfellow's *Hiawatha*, and spoke a kind word for Miss Sewell's novel *Cleve Hall*, which he rated above *Margaret Percival* as less dogmatic and sectarian. He developed principles, sociological rather than esthetic, such as that "a successful Phi Beta Kappa poem is an impossibility".[14]

By all odds Hale's most significant review of vital creative literature was his greeting in January 1856 of Walt Whitman's *Leaves of Grass*. Unnoticed at the time, it received its due praise with the growth of Whitman's fame as the first favorable published review of *Leaves of Grass*, aside from those written by Whitman himself. That Hale praised Whitman's work, despite the temperamental chasm between the two men, is less remarkable than that he praised it for so many of the right reasons. The directness of the language amazed Hale no less than the poet's profound understanding of the American spirit. "The wonderful sharpness and distinctness of his imagination" has produced "thumb-nail sketches . . . so real that we wonder how they came on paper"(277).[15]

After the 1850s, Hale wrote little for the *North American Review* until 1880. Meanwhile, the format and the policy of the magazine had been modernized in that articles were now signed and less directly dependent on current books. Hale, who had also changed, was now speaking as a minister and was exercising the privilege of a wise elder. His formal articles between 1880 and 1894 are characteristic statements of his well-known attitudes, for he expressed them many times in his lectures. The principal subjects are religion, education, and citizenship; and the first two are indispensable for the third. Solid without becoming heavy, they urge more efficient schools and greater attention to local government.[16]

Although Hale was not an important enough writer in 1857 to have been solicited for a contribution to the first number of the *Atlantic*, he was an influential prepublication supporter and sponsor. As a close friend of Moses Phillips, the publisher, he was a useful man in the background, as Phillips revealed in a later statement to William Sloane Kennedy: "Mr. Phillips used to say [Kennedy wrote] that if it had not been for his [Hale's] interest he would not have undertaken the magazine".[17] Hale, who soon became a contributor also, began with a modest personal essay, "The Dot and

Line Alphabet" (October 1858), and continued with a successful story, "My Double and How He Undid Me" (1859), which was much cleverer after Lowell's drastic excisions than in Hale's original version. As one of the second class contributors, he provided miscellaneous sketches until *The Man Without a Country* (December 1863); after its publication, he became a desirable contributor and, when the original policy of anonymity was reversed, a name with drawing power.

Hale remained a regular if infrequent contributor to the *Atlantic* until the establishment in 1870 of his own competing magazine *Old and New*. His best contributions included "The Queen of California," the leading article for March 1864[18]; one of his many tributes to Edward Everett (March 1865); and the series on Sybaris from 1867 and 1868. When he resumed writing for the magazine, he contributed a genial account of the early history of Phi Beta Kappa (July 1879); a pair of indecisive biblical sketches (January and March 1882); and a note on the shipwreck episode near the beginning of *Robinson Crusoe* (July 1885). More valuable were the graceful reminiscences of his childhood and youth that were collected as *A New England Boyhood* (1892).

Undoubtedly Hale's writing for the *Atlantic* brought him more fame, and presumably more fortune, than his writing for the *North American Review*. It proved his versatility beyond reporting and interpreting current events and publications. The distinguished editors helped him develop his prankish sense of humor. Unfortunately they also encouraged one of his worst habits—a tendency toward trifling, genteel space filling.[19] Hale's publications in the *North American Review* reveal a sturdier character, a more earnest citizen with a deeper insight into social trends.

Files of the *Outlook*, his principal medium for the last decade of his life, indicate another aspect of his many-sided character. Hale had written as early as 1871 and 1872 for its predecessor, the *Christian Union*, both fiction ("Alice MacNeil's Christmas Tree" and "Water Talk") and religious articles ("Prayer") when it was supervised by Henry Ward Beecher. In addition to the three series that became full length books, Hale wrote numerous single articles of reminiscence for the *Outlook*, as well as reports on Unitarian conferences (October 6, 1894) and peace conferences (June 22, 1895, and February 25, 1899) that were fully abreast of the times. His continued skill with book reviewing was demonstrated by his discussion of Frederick W. Holl's *Peace Conference at the Hague* (April 20 and 27, 1901) in which he distinguished between the English word *armament* and the French *armement* to argue in favor of limitation as a more practical proposal than elimination.

A feature of the *Outlook* was an occasional symposium on a literary subject. Hale took part in several, selecting "The Greatest Books of the Century" (December 1, 1900), "The Best Books for Children" (December 7, 1901), and the books most characteristically American in "A Complete Picture" (December 6, 1902). He also joined in discussions of "The Creative Spirit in Literature: Is It Dead or Dormant?" (November 24, 1906) and "Literature or Life" (November 23, 1907), in which the question was the contrast between fiction and newspapers.

Few of Hale's answers to these questions should have been unexpected. Most surprising from him is the place of Goethe at the head of his list as a man who made a mark on the century with *Faust* and *Wilhelm Meister*. "One is glad to see that the century is rubbing the mark out," Hale wrote, "but, all the same, the mark was there."[20] On the more speculative topic relative to books that were likely to endure, Hale virtually declined committing himself, knowing that on this subject young women would be better prophets than old men. There was no hesitancy, however, in his statements about the survival of a reading public. In "Not Less Read but Different Standards," the title of his discussion, his evidence was statistical and historical; for he contrasted the five "literary journals" that had met the demands of the minority "reading class" in 1841 with the eighty-five published in New York in 1907 with a sale of four million copies a month. A "reading class" had grown into "the people," who read "at least fifty times as much fiction"—and everything else in print.[21]

IV   Old and New, *1870–1875*

Hale's ambition to publish the universal ideal literary magazine led to the greatest journalistic disappointment of his life, the failure of *Old and New*. This publication was not his only magazine, neither his first nor last, but it was the darling of his heart. During the five years of its existence, it absorbed a tremendous amount of his energy, for he took personal charge of every aspect—financing, physical makeup, scouting for contributors, writing, proofreading, and promoting sales. Sponsored partly by the Unitarian Association, it came as near as anything could to inciting ill will among friends.[22] When it was absorbed by *Scribner's*, saddened as Hale felt at the failure of his dream, he found relief from harrowing minor responsibilities. His next effort, after a decade, *Lend A Hand: A Journal of Organized Philanthropy* (vol. I, no. 1., January 1886), was more modest, in keeping within the limits set by its title, and it was proportionately more successful in operation.

Old and New suffered from Hale's attempt to please everybody; it began with entertainment for the children of a family—for whom he wrote a parody serial story, *John Whopper, the Newsboy*[23]—and simultaneously contained other articles "profound enough for the most metaphysical, or learned enough for the most learned of the household." This intention is an ideal which, he confessed, is difficult to reach; and his efforts fell farther short of it than he admitted. In an engaging parody review of the first issue that Hale published in the second, he recognized that "there is good writing in it, that is certain, and there is bad writing in it, that is certain." The fatal weakness, however, was the attempt to promote a multitude of good works in a single package of entertainment and education and to wrap all in the liberal theology demanded by the Unitarian Association.

From the beginning Hale received contributions from notable writers: the first volume published verse by Harriet Beecher Stowe, travel notes by Julia Ward Howe, articles by James Freeman Clarke, Henry W. Bellows, Washington Gladden, and Henry James, Sr. Among less well remembered writers, he had Paul Hayne, the Georgia poet; Lucretia P. Hale; Gail Hamilton; and Mrs. A. D. T. Whitney. In later volumes, pieces appeared by John Muir, John Burroughs, Charles Dudley Warner, James Martineau, Oliver Wendell Holmes, and others of equal stature. One of the serials was Mrs. Stowe's *Pink and White Tyranny*, which began in August 1870 and ended in August 1871. Another serial, which began in December 1871, was written in "co-partnership" by Mrs. Stowe, Hale, Mrs. Whitney, Miss Hale, and two nonprofessionals.

Both the fiction and the verse, including Hale's own, were generally poor, but the regular departments were of high quality. Hale wrote unsigned reviews in "The Examiner" and news notes in the "Record of Progress" with his customary skill and intelligence, and he solicited equally good treatments from Clarke (for example, Joseph Ernest Renan's *Saint Paul*) and others (for example, James's

Secret of Swedenborg, reviewed by David A. Wasson). These sober, substantial articles were possibly a bit more dull than the standard of writing in the *Atlantic* or in the *North American Review*, but a large number of lively articles also appeared about tariff regulations, industrial cooperatives, prison reform, and other interests of the editor and his likeminded contributors.

Unsigned literary notes from early issues included a tribute to Benjamin Disraeli on the prospects for a new novel; obituary tributes to Charles Dickens; and a welcome to a "new" poet, Dante Gabriel Rossetti. The primarily didactic approach to literature—which Hale shared—dominated detailed discussions of "The Modern English Novel" by Henry W. Bellows, and recent "American Poetry" by William B. Weeden.[24] Among recent poets, Hale's close friend Weeden had particularly harsh words for Joaquin Miller, whose verse was called "vile" and whose "Kit Carson's Ride" infuriated him: "A more selfish egotism we may search all printed pages to find, and come back empty-handed; selfish in that it is so petty." Although Weeden's attitude is more conciliatory toward John Hay, Harte, and Whitman, he found none of them equal to either Longfellow or Lowell.

Of the many reasons for the failure of magazines, the primary one is always inability to attract enough paying readers to cover expenses. In *Old and New*, the old was not conservative enough for people who mistrusted Hippolyte Taine and Renan, but the new was not in step with the generation of Mark Twain and Henry James. Hale's editorial judgment was not infallible: he rejected a manuscript submitted by Sarah Orne Jewett, and he declined the American rights to Bulwer Lytton's fantastic Utopian *The Coming Race*, which attained more popularity than any material in Hale's magazine. He relied too heavily on his personal prestige; for, though he could expect support for his social proposals and could be sure of receptive readers for his lighter writings, few readers could accept the whole package month after month.[25]

CHAPTER 7

Practical Ethics

I *The Duty of Responsible Citizenship*

A S a Christian minister, Dr. Hale had more opportunities than
most men to scatter advice indiscriminately; but he restrained
himself more successfully than most men do. By profession, he was
required to help his parishioners solve their and their children's
moral problems. This duty he considered to be one to be performed
to the best of his ability—but upon request. Later he transmitted his
notes and observations to the larger groups who bought magazines,
listened to lectures, and enrolled in study courses—also upon the
request of editors and lyceum bureaus.

Such is the background of two books of moral advice, *How to Do
It* (1871) and *How to Live*, which were reissued together in 1900 as
the seventh volume of Hale's *Works*. The first of these originated in
articles for *Our Young Folks* and the *Youth's Companion*, and they
were ostensibly for adolescent boys and girls. The second, ostensibly for adults, consisted of rewritten Lowell Institute lectures from
1869 about "The Divine Method in Human Life," revised seventeen
years later for the Chautauqua Reading Course. The segregation of
readers by age is not significant, for the advice is based upon the
same appeal to reason. The topics are either the same—reading,
study, social responsibility, churchgoing—or are as deliberately
parallel, as "Life with Your Elders" in one of the books and "How to
Deal with One's Children" in the other.

Hale was seldom dogmatic, but he was usually explicit. In the
chapters on "how to talk," his advice to adolescents was conveyed in
capital letters, large size:

TELL THE TRUTH
DO NOT TALK ABOUT YOUR OWN AFFAIRS
CONFESS IGNORANCE

TALK TO THE PERSON WHO IS TALKING TO YOU
NEVER UNDERRATE YOUR INTERLOCUTOR
BE SHORT.

These are principles which, embellished with literary references to
Maria Edgeworth and personal references to "Mr." Alexander Agas-
siz, are sufficiently sound to bear repetition.

The companion volume for elders, *How to Live*, is equally in
touch with reality; for Hale makes no claim for universal wisdom or
for validity outside a group selected by nationality, economic position, and ideology. "This is an American book, written by an American author for American readers. . . . an American who is neither
rich nor poor, for Americans who are neither rich nor poor" (200–
201) and who "believe in the existence of God, and in his presence
here now"(198).

Within a framework so definitely recognized, most of the advice is
more applicable to the Chautauquans of 1886 than to their highly
urbanized descendants. Even so, some of Hale's tenets are unexpected. For example, his insistence on sleep as a matter of ethics:
"To sleep well is one of your duties. . . . You must sleep well, if you
mean to do the rest well"(211). Sleeping regularly, soundly, and
enough is as necessary to the ethically good life as abstention from
intoxicating liquors, and for much the same reasons. Only on the
basis of such personal habits can a person fulfill the higher duties of
serving God and the commonwealth.

A third book of advice on how to live, *What Career?* (1878),
centers on the opportunities and responsibilities of education outside of and beyond schools as well as in them. Whatever a person's
bread-and-butter occupation may be, Hale assured his readers, systematic study throughout life—he advocated two hours daily—is as
indispensable as wholesome food and adequate rest, horseback riding, swimming, or battledore and shuttlecock. Hale's conception of
the well-spent life was clear. His major heroes were men who
influenced history—Benjamin Franklin, George Washington—and
whose achievements were a source of spiritual sustenance. Not far
below them in his estimation were inventors of useful tools and
appliances—Robert Fulton, Eli Whitney—who contributed notably
to the public welfare. Honorable public servants—John Quincy
Adams, Daniel Webster—and well-oriented writers—Whittier,
Dickens, Elizabeth Barrett Browning—were also examples of the
better life to whom Hale frequently alluded.

In addressing ordinary men, however, Hale avoided the excessive optimism of telling everyone that he had within himself the makings of a major hero. Though any man can face adversity, within his limits, with the courage of Washington, or emulate the ingenuity of Franklin or the eloquence of Webster—and the more credit to him if he does—good character will not make him a Washington. Man's resolving to hitch his wagon to a star would not guarantee his getting there. Better than such personal ambition is his consistent willingness to "lend a hand," for the result is the certainty of becoming that first rate civic asset, the good citizen.[1]

II   *Ante-bellum Issues: Popular Sovereignty and the Melting Pot*

From infancy, Hale was introduced as naturally into the world of business and government as into the world of books. Unlike his contemporaries from ministerial families, he needed no sudden revelation of financial fluctuations and political pressures. From boyhood, he was prepared for dual citizenship in the realm of affairs no less than that of ideas; the newspaper office, his second college, was an unexcelled training ground for pamphleteering. The exact date at which he became aware that he needed systematic reading in social problems is not known, but he did so early in the years of his first pastorate. His son suggests 1847 as a time of intensive study of emigration, taxation, poor relief, and delinquency, but it is clear that a sense of his deficiency had been growing upon him for several years previously.

The first issue upon which Hale took a public stand was the admission in 1845 of Texas to the Union. At the time of annexation, he was twenty-three years old, and was already confirmed in his opposition to the extension of slavery. As a resident of Washington during a winter of legislative debates for and against annexation, he had been a constant listener at the capitol and a source of information for the *Advertiser*. On leaving for home, he asked Rufus Choate, the Massachusetts senator, what he should report to his father. Replied the senator, *"Magno proelio victi sumus"*; in other words, "we are beaten" (*Works*, VI, 220). With the optimism of youth Hale, though "wild with the excitement of defeat"(220), refused to submit without a struggle. He wrote a pamphlet, paid to have it printed, and offered it for sale at five cents a copy. Though nobody bought it in 1845, Hale recalled, he thought well enough of it in 1900 to reprint it in his selected *Works* (VI, 221–36) as *Freedom in Texas*, an abridgement of his original title, *How to Conquer Texas before Texas Conquers Us: A Tract for the Times.*

Hale's prescription was, as he observed, the same that he applied later to the settlement of Kansas: the mass migration of Northern antislavery men into the territory. No great material sacrifice would be involved, for the population was sparse, the land was excellent for grazing, and the area was "one of the finest agricultural countries in the world"(224). It offered similar opportunities for real estate development, and its climate and natural resources contained "a thousand advantages which neither Michigan, nor Wisconsin, nor Iowa, nor Illinois can offer." His conclusion was that "it is not wild nor Utopian to hope that, by a systematic and united effort, free emigration, and free labor, and free institutions may attain a predominance in this territory" (*Works*, VI, 226). An expanded version of these views appeared in 1854, in Hale's book *Kanzas and Nebraska*, with a greatly improved program for getting results.

Hale's book on Kansas (which he insisted on spelling *Kanzas*) and Nebraska is partly historical, but it was basically a publicity effort in support of "popular sovereignty" as promoted by the Massachusetts Emigrant Aid Company founded in the spring of 1854. Its thesis was straightforward: if Kansas and Nebraska were to be admitted as either free or slave states by popular vote of the settlers, a strenuous effort should be made to encourage mass emigration from the free states. The inducements offered by Hale on behalf of the company were varied. They included a glamorous description of the territories, an optimistic appraisal of their potentialities for profitable development, and substantial financial assistance to settlers through group rates and long-term loans. With these practical considerations Hale mingled ethical appeals; and he became so abstract that he predicted that the company's stockholders would "receive that satisfaction, ranked by Lord Bacon among the very highest, of becoming founders of states and, more than this, states which are prosperous and free"(226–27).

Though Hale had no premonition of the subsequent guerilla warfare of "bleeding Kansas" or of the displacement of nonviolent penetration by Beecher Bibles,[2] he could never be completely a booster. He was skeptical of the speedy construction of a transcontinental railroad; and he was also disturbed, though insufficiently, by the "anything but agreeable" question of how to avoid mistreatment of the Indian population(58).

In spite of its lapses, *Kanzas and Nebraska* was a fine compilation
of material for use in 1854. Hale had read carefully, as stated in his
preface, the memoirs of the first French travelers; the later reports
of Zebulon Pike, Benjamin Bonneville, John Charles Fremont, and
others less remembered; the writings of Francis Parkman and Albert Gallatin; the records of legislative debates and other official
documents—everything available, in short, including newspaper articles to the date of publication. The result justified his modest
self-satisfaction: "Working with the disadvantages of a first collector,
I have simply tried to make this book accurate as far as it goes"(v). As
the earliest book written on Kansas, it has special attractions for
Kansan antiquarians; and the original manuscript is fittingly preserved in the collection of the Kansas Historical Society in Topeka.

Though a less inclusive and a less emotionally dangerous topic
than the extension or elimination of black slavery, Hale's sixty-four
page pamphlet *Letters on Irish Emigration* (1852) concerns more
than the Irish and the date of publication; for the flood of im-
poverished Irish immigrants created an emergency, and racial tensions, important to several Eastern cities, notably Boston. Unlike
Hale's book on Kansas that urged his readers to act as individuals,
his analysis of immigration was primarily a reporting assignment
that was to advocate action by the national government. By combin-
ing assertions of the material and ethical benefits of immigration,
Hale displayed his public spirit at the age of thirty as well as his
journalistic skill. Beyond this work's contemporary relevance, it is a
thoughtful view of problems of racial assimilation that became increasingly serious through the years with the succeeding waves of
refugees yet to come in the second half of the century:

The State should stop at once its effort to sweep them back. . . . It should
welcome them; register them; send them at once to the labor-needing
regions; care for them if sick; and end, by a system, all that mass of unsys-
tematic statute which handles them as outcasts or Pariahs. . . . and Nation,
State, or man should feel that the Emigration is the greatest instead of the
least element of our material prosperity; an element which should brace us
to meet and handle any difficulties, real or fancied, which it may bring to
our institutions of politics or of religion.(58)[3]

III   *The New Civilization*

Although Hale, who was neither an egoist nor a dreamer, was a
prodigious worker, his later discussions of public affairs are mostly

minor variations in support of the causes with which he was preoc-
cupied. Instead of elaborate pamphlets or extended explanations, he
wrote notes. His ideas were firm and consistent enough, and careful
surveys of his writings would produce compilations of parallel utter-
ances from his fiction, his sermons, lectures, and magazine articles
on most public issues of his time, but no central treatment. "The
New Civilization" itself—a phrase that Hale appears to have coined
toward the end of the Civil War—gradually assumed a wider meaning to him than Reconstruction of the South, for it eventually included all the domestic reforms that he advocated.

The selection that Hale made for Volume VIII of his *Works*,
called *Addresses and Essays*, is far from a balanced sampling of his
thinking. Of the three sections into which the book is divided, the
most unified is that on education, which occupies the first third; and
the least satisfactory section is that on sociology, which includes
papers from the 1850s and the 1890s. Between these two groups
that relate to the new civilization is a section unconnected with it,
"History and Biography." This section contains his affectionate tribute to Emerson (1893) and antiquarian lore on "Puritan Politics in
England and New England" (1869), "The People's Battle" (1893)—
Bunker Hill, "the beginning of the People's victory"—and "The
Contributions of Boston to American Independence" (1897).

One of Hale's best papers on elementary education, a *North
American Review* article from 1883, "Half-time in Schools," was
unfortunately not reprinted in his *Works*, though it developed a
topic important to him.[4] Schools abused pupils, he knew, by wast-
ing time on subjects better learned at home—like how to make a
bed or broil a beefsteak—and they made drudgery out of what
should be recreation—like reading Scott's *Ivanhoe*. As a substitute
for miseducation, he recommended shortened school terms that
emphasized basic disciplines and left free time for practical experience and individualized recreation. Pungently expressed in his best
style, his thesis was that the schooling of a Daniel Webster or of a
Jonathan Edwards is as desirable for the present and the future as it
was in old New England: three months in the winter and a summer
term, with intelligent amateur teachers like Lucretia Garfield, Harriet Beecher, and Edward Everett. Hale wrapped up his discourse
with the Yankee thought that half-time schooling, in addition to its
educational advantages, costs the taxpayer only half as much as
full-time enrollment.

Public service and public responsibility are the themes of the papers in Volume VIII called "Sociology." As early as 1853 he wrote "The State's Care of Its Children Considered as a Check on Juvenile Delinquency," in which he recommended that parents who could not control their children should have them committed to "Receiving Homes," reform schools in which they would get expert preparation for constructive living. In "Public Amusement for Poor and Rich" (1857), he maintained that recreation, as necessary as work, merits civic support.

Two much later papers illustrate the extension and limitations of Hale's advocacy of public ownership. He was neither a doctrinaire Socialist nor an all-out supporter of private business. Some property should be private, he explained to the Boston Society for Citizenship (1888), but not all. "Good libraries, good pavements, good amusements, good hospitals, are opened by the common wealth to all (*Works*, VIII, 403), a great empire to be preserved for future generations. In 1894, talking to the Bellamy First Nationlist Club of Boston on "New England Nationalism" (that is, *nationalization*), he was equally specific in his justification of such government-owned or regulated enterprises as highways and post offices. "The principle seems to be this: wherever something is needed for every member of the community . . . it is desirable that the community shall provide this requisite"(388–89).

These ideas were familiar enough to the original audience, for Hale had expressed them with similar distinctness in an earlier article for their magazine, *The Nationalist*. His title and subject, "The Best Government," was the reverse of the "old saw" about governing least; for his "best" government does the most for its citizens by providing roads and mail deliveries, by permitting municipal ownership of public utilities, or by doing whatever else would benefit the public. "The question is simply a question of cheapness," he wrote, "the merest matter of practical expense and convenience."[5]

The full extension of Hale's new civilization is hard to state definitely, for Hale was inclined to imply approval of views contrary to his own if he thought them to be honestly and constructively intended. The lend-a-hand periodicals are his record of proposals but not of unreserved endorsement. A convenient approximate guide to main parts of his new civilization is provided by his unreprinted contributions to the *Cosmopolitan* between 1889 and 1892, particularly to a monthly department on "Social Problems." These brief informal statements, expressed in his persuasive personal style, define his major aims: peace in the world, cooperation within the nation, humanization of the city, and education of the person. Specific proposals suggested by current happenings are his examples of what can be done, but these recommendations do not make a complete program of reform.

Hale favored lowering postage rates on books (as has been done) and nationalizing the telegraph (as has not). He approved self-education clubs for women and American Culture courses in colleges, both of which have to some degree come into being; but his hope for more impartial discussion of government than by political oratory and the mass media has yet to be realized. He could find no good in gambling, whether through the Louisiana Lottery or at the Court of King James; but he was more tolerant of alcoholism. Denouncing distillers and grog shops, he knew, could produce neither abstinence nor temperance: "You overcome evil by putting in good"—innocent stimulants and family drinking parlors.[6]

His position about two restless minorities, women and workingmen, was conservative. The best place for women, he was certain, was in the home, in spite of the current "transition stage in which curious experiments are tried".[7] For the workingman, he favored three-way cooperation with capital and management, not conflict between organized labor and ownership. In his scheme of things, there were no permanent economic classes. In an inclusive discussion of the labor question, he wrote that "the object to be aimed at is the steady promotion of all drudges to the ranks of intelligent work"; and he commended Edward Bellamy for his suggestion—an anticipation of William James's moral equivalent for war—that young men be drafted for two or three years for "muscular work" in preparation for "higher services."[8]

One of Hale's last books, "We, the People" (1903), a volume impressive for the psychological modernity of its octogenarian author, is an elaboration of his continued advocacy of responsible citizenship. Taking as his title the first three words of the preamble to the national Constitution, Hale added the descriptive phrase, "A Series of Papers on Topics of To-day." The book is composed of fifty-one short articles, most of them about a thousand words each, and of three longer pieces; and none of them were written before 1901. Thirty-nine of the short articles were reprinted from the New York

American, to which they had been contributed, on invitation from William Randolph Hearst, during the autumn of 1902. They are signed editorials that Hale called "leaders," using the old term, but that would now be called "columns." The remaining short articles are editorials of the same period from the *Christian Register* and the *Lend a Hand Record.* The longer pieces are a magazine article from the *Cosmopolitan* and commencement addresses at Ohio State University (1901) and Smith College (1902).

Hale was still an accomplished journalist, always earnest and never pompous, as guiltless of splitting hairs as infinitives. His most important suggestion was to broaden the scope of collective ownership. Although he sometimes sounded like Norman Thomas, he was indignant when old "grumblers," living by Adam Smith or the *Nation,* called him an Anarchist, a Socialist, or a Jacobin (*"We, the People"*, 62). His objection was justified, for the term "public ownership" as he used it is not limited to ownership by the national government. As Hale used "public," it often became equivalent to "cooperative." Any nonprofit group, such as a tax-free church, was public in his sense, and so was a cooperative building society. A motion passed by a town meeting or an award made by an academy for the arts is as much an act of the people and as public within its restricted sphere as legislation by Congress. Hale advocated group insurance (as sponsored by fraternal organizations), consumer cooperatives, and profit-sharing small industries—all of them "public"—as forms of mutual aid.

The posthumous collection called *Mohonk Addresses* (1910) presents Hale's last words on international relations and world peace, thus paralleling *"We, the People,"* the expression of his final attitudes toward domestic politics and national economy. The two subjects were closely related, for Hale's new civilization demanded an improved standard of living at home because physical security was accompanied by a heightened moral sense—a combination possible only in a peaceful world. If his concept of American leadership was sometimes more nearly imperialistic than altruistic, his thinking was never isolationist or hostile to the integrity of other nations.

As Hale was neither a pacifist nor a visionary, his proposals for peace emphasized practical measures that might lead to permanent results. Although he did not disdain having ad hoc arbitration commissions settle single disputes, or arms limitation agreements between pairs of nations, he regretted their lack of lasting effect as well as their limited scope. Regional agreements, such as a Pan-American pact, or international conferences like those at Geneva and The Hague, appeared far superior to Hale because they could incorporate principles and procedures applicable to tensions and problems before they reached the acute crisis stage. He advocated, therefore, a world court, a permanent tribunal, that was to be established by the world powers and to which disputes between nations could be referred—if and only if the litigants wished.[9] He rejected compulsory arbitration as visionary and, as he wrote Theodore Roosevelt in 1901, "absurd almost in name, when you come to states [nations]." Decisions of the court would be supported solely by their justice, not by a world government or by an international army (*Life and Letters*, II, 386).

Hale had no faith in a league of nations. He described the familiar poetic ideal of the "parliament of man, the federation of the world" as "the Utopia of a Tennyson" (*Mohonk Addresses*, 45); and he quoted with approval a contrasting legal epigram, "We have too many parliaments, and we do not have enough courts"(12). He believed also that governments have too many diplomats, "twitching and pulling and fixing and fussing"(24), for "the old diplomacy is not up to the rapidity of our time"(48). Once the probity of a court is acknowledged, however, "when the decision is made by an impartial Tribunal which says 'This is justice,' the world will attend, the press will sweep around into line, and the pulpit will speak the words of infinite truth if it knows them"(28).

It is easy, no doubt, a half century and more later, to recognize the deficiencies of proposals like Hale's. They had been made before, as he knew, by Henri IV of France in the sixteenth century and by William Penn in the seventeenth. The lessons of 1914, 1939, and later, bitter as they have been, support rather than diminish Hale's warning against the alternative: "In whatever position we are placed, we are to remember that this world cannot come to its bearings, does not understand the use of the science it has been creating in the last century, unless it finds out that the human race is but one individual, and that we are so many separate leaves and twigs on the bough of the tree, each of us having a contribution which he is to render for the good of all"(65).

CHAPTER 8

Sermons

I *Religious Principles*

ALTHOUGH Hale's religious beliefs changed little during the decades of his ministry, his expression became less systematic and formal in later years. In the same way that his early novel *Margaret Percival in America* (1850) is more theological than his later fiction, he as a young preacher felt an obligation to explain ideas for his congregation but he was more concerned later with developing attitudes and encouraging actions. Hale at his most theological appears in his first published collection, a series of five doctrinal sermons delivered early in 1860.

Issued under the title *The Elements of Christian Doctrine and its Development*,[1] its special character resulted from occurrences in Boston that deeply disturbed and pained Hale. His friend Dr. Frederic Huntington, his immediate predecessor as minister at the South Congregational Church, had resigned his important professorship at Harvard University and joined the Episcopal Church. Hale considered this a backward step historically and as unfaithfulness to the progressive doctrines that he wanted his congregation to accept. For this reason, he introduced polemical material that he ordinarily shunned, such as sparring with current theologians (the debate running over into footnotes), citations of church fathers, and wholesale biblical quotations. Arranged by Hale with the polemicist's outline of statement, definition, analysis, and rebuttal, they resemble a formal exercise for an examining board of skeptical critics.

Unlike Hale's later sermons as these are in manner, the doctrines in this pamphlet—for it is only that in spite of its imposing title—are consistent with those of his maturity that "the test of a belief in Christ is the following Christ"(29) and that "the Christianity of every

93

generation ought to be on a higher plane than that of the generation before"(46). In Hale's version of church history, an upward progression from plane to plane began in Europe with the rejection of compulsory ritual and with liberation from the authoritarian rule of bishops. To these achievements, brought to New England by the Pilgrim Fathers, he added the replacement of the harsh insistence on man's sinfulness by the kindlier interpretation of mankind that reached a peak in the humanism of William Ellery Channing and other liberal theologians of the early nineteenth century. These views, which constituted a widely held position within the Congregational churches around Boston and Cambridge, were a progressive midpoint between the old Calvinism and ultramodern Transcendentalism.

The unnatural verbal dexterity of Hale's important public address or "Election" sermon of 1859 suggests that he may have been in more doubt at that time about the functions of his ministry than about his beliefs. The occasion for its delivery was the kind of civic distinction in which he took great pleasure, as he made evident when he reprinted his speech in the sixth volume of his *Works* (370–98) as "A Sermon Delivered before Governor Banks, the Lieutenant-Governor, the Council, and the General Court, January 5, 1859."

Appealing to the history of the commonwealth, Hale attempted to persuade the legislators that the legal separation of church and state, which had occurred in Massachusetts twenty-five years previously, implied full cooperation in social amelioration, not a division of responsibility. The citizens who elect a senator or a governor are, unless they fail to vote, the same who elect a deacon or a bishop unless they exclude themselves from church affairs. Their identical business in both functions is to serve the people: the lawmakers to "deal with men in general, as organized in society"; the churchmen to counsel and guide the individual, the exceptional(391). The legislature properly attempts to prevent *pauperism* "in the abstract"(392), but the minister cannot practice the "stoic cruelty" of letting a starving woman die in order to justify the law against begging.

Such subtle legal distinctions, not far removed from sophistry, disappear as Hale specifies the major duties of the government of Massachusetts, "administrator of the largest single system of Christian charities in the world"(379). Major these duties were in 1859, and major they remain today—to extend welfare and education and to improve the administration of courts and prisons: "the reform of 14,000 criminals yearly; the cure of a thousand lunatics and idiots; the reception of 10,000 exiles; the finding eyes for all the blind, and ears for all the deaf, and tongues for all the dumb; the education of 200,000 children, and the expenditure of a million for the poor"(379). Noting as a "very ugly symptom"(385) the growth of crime in Massachusetts at the rate of six to one over population, Hale asked, "Where is it we have fallen short?"—a question in which the *we* included the church and the state.

After the Civil War, Hale answered religious questions positively for the huge auxiliary congregation reached through the prestige of his writings. An example of how his ideas extended to larger groups is shown by the distribution of an essay which was originally spoken as a sermon preached in his church on May 8, 1881, under the title "The Unitarian Principles." He printed it in the same year in the collection of his sermons, *June to May*. It was then reprinted for wider distribution by the American Unitarian Association (fourth series, no. 51). A few years later it was supplemented by an article, "Why Am I a Unitarian?", for the *North American Review*, for which Hale incorporated material from the original sermon and rearranged it for an interdenominational audience.

No appreciable doctrinal significance attaches to Hale's designation as Congregationalist before the Civil War and usually as Unitarian after 1865. From beginning to end, he was both a Congregationalist and an Unitarian; for, at that time, there was no contradiction between the two terms. By long tradition, the Congregational body was independent in the extreme; for each local church selected the minister of its choice, according to its preference for fundamental Calvinism or revisionism. The Unitarians, or *liberals*, as they preferred to be known, became one wing, as it were, so different in emphasis from the more conventional preaching of a Henry Ward Beecher that in 1865 and 1866 leaders called national conventions of Unitarian Congregationalists to establish an organized Unitarian Association. Hale, one of the leaders, was a chief lieutenant of Henry W. Bellows and thus one of the creators of the Unitarian Church; but the new name implied no angry break with the past and no dramatic rejection of his former attitudes and convictions.[2]

A striking feature of Hale's unitarianism, shown clearly in both the tract and the magazine article, is the difference between his definition of his key word and that in common use. *Unitarian* in his sense is not, he explains, primarily a doctrine in opposition to *trinitarian;* instead, it is an appeal for agreement within the entire Christian church upon essential aims and attitudes. "For myself, I can attend the service of the Roman Church with pleasure and profit," he explains. "If I find myself in a Catholic town in Europe, where there is no Protestant Church, I always go to worship with the Catholics."[3] The word *unitarian*, uncapitalized, is therefore related in its root to *unitary* and in meaning to our current *ecumenical*. The same word capitalized designates a denomination, the Unitarian Church of America, with an independent organization and a special interpretation of the humanity of Jesus, the son of God.

Hale never felt a conflict between these two uses of the term, for his principles embraced both meanings equally. Because he rejects all efforts to compel complete agreement among Christians, his principles do not include a formalized creed or "any authoritative statement of form or dogma."[4] His belief rests primarily upon the New Testament, since Jesus, as "an exhibition of perfect manhood" is the greatest of teachers, but not to the exclusion of Spinoza or Plato, Buddha or Confucius, Augustine or John Wesley, all of whom were also children of God and sharers in the revelation of God's fatherhood: "From all these convictions it follows as a matter of necessity that the Unitarian Church demands purity of character from those who belong to it. Strictly speaking, this is all that it demands. It asks for other things; but character is essential."[5]

The *North American Review* article is more specific. Ritualistic ceremonies and theological formulas are at best picturesque relics, he says; and such beliefs as total depravity and the "horrible dogma about hell" are barbarous. Only faith, hope, and love are indispensable: "Faith in God, Hope of Heaven, and Love of Man."[6] The precise forms of worship permit "eclecticism" since man's duties are to follow Jesus and do God's will on earth. In contrast to adherents of backward-looking creeds, the Unitarians and other liberal Christians live for the present and the future, fully committed to the Kingdom of God as promised by the Father to his children.

Hale was never ambitious enough to take executive leadership of his denomination. Until the death of Bellows in 1882, Hale was content to serve as his assistant. To the end of his life, he attended church conferences regularly, spoke his mind freely, and reported the proceedings with professional expertness; but he had no urge to control such meetings. Outside the denomination, on the other hand, he became the best known Unitarian minister in the United States, a public symbol of the faith.[7]

II *Sermons, 1878–1881*

Hale expressed regret for his inability to select thirty or more sermons to include in his *Works*. He never found time, he said, to sort through the fifteen hundred in manuscript. This excuse, which was only partly valid, led to the explanation that "a sermon, from its nature, may well be regarded as ephemeral" *(Works,* X, vii*)*. The four or five million words which he estimated were his to select from had already served their purpose—or so he hoped. Actually, his sermons have more lasting value than the mediocre verses that replaced them. The sermons were well written, they have an idiomatic directness of phrase unlike the florid eloquence of other popular pulpit orators; and they contain progressive suggestions that have become—or are in the process of becoming—accepted outside the small liberal circle of a century ago.

Hale's apologies for his sermons should not be taken literally, and he certainly did not mean to limit his audience to listeners at his church. They were written to be read as well as heard; and, after the demise of *Old and New* in 1875, many sermons were regularly printed as pamphlets and distributed each week by mail. From time to time groups were gathered, bound in hard covers, and sold as books. Six volumes appeared within a two year period under such titles as *From Thanksgiving to Fast* (1879) and *June to May* (1881).[8] As personal expressions, these Sunday exercises parallel the magazine articles and secular lectures gathered into such books as *How To Do It* and *How To Live;* yet the form and the illustrative examples show differentiating characteristics that are suited to pulpit delivery.

The range of subjects and the structural similarities among Hale's sermons are evidence enough that he composed them with a closer adherence to theory than in his happy-go-lucky fictional fables. Trial and error helped him devise a pattern he liked, for he was critically observant of models—especially sermons he heard in youth—and by good fortune he inherited a formula from a distinguished predecessor in the profession. In *June to May* he refers to his ideal of craftsmanship in the sermon "These Three Abide."

Hale notes in it as "substantially true" a statement by an older colleague—Ephraim Peabody, who died in 1856—that only eight subjects exist for sermons. Hale lists them, by his own analysis, as God, heaven, and "our relations to man"; the virtues of faith, hope, and Christian love; the intertwining of some or all of these six; and finally, direct applications for individual or social improvement. Besides these subjects, there are substitutes for sermons in addresses appropriate for Sunday services, about personal experiences, cultural topics, and current events. Once a young preacher has presented the eight basic subjects, Hale agreed with Ephraim Peabody, he could only do so again, repeatedly, but better than before.

Hale's practice was consistent with Ephraim Peabody's and his own advice. Among the twenty-six sermons in *June to May*, seven are primarily doctrinal, corresponding to Peabody's first three subjects. Another seven deal with Peabody's next trio of subjects, the basic Christian virtues of faith, hope, and love. Four are definite instruction in practical individual ethics, and the remaining eight are addresses on current topics, literary and cultural or sociological and political. In almost all of them, the intertwining of doctrine and application is explicit; and even the most limited, such as an appeal for support of the Boston Associated Charities or opposition to a proposed statute change relaxing restrictions on Sunday labor, invoke moral and religious principles.

The materials that Hale used to develop his topics can be similarly assigned to a few broad categories. Four sermons are composed mainly of biblical examples, another four of examples from United States or world history, and those in a third quartet are comparative. Three sermons are straightforward discussions of current problems of urban life, pauperism the most obvious; and another three are literary discussions. Among these the obituary address on Thomas Carlyle, which is at this later date the most genuinely readable contribution to *June to May*, is an enthusiastic appreciation of Carlyle's *Sartor Resartus*.

In the majority of these sermons, Hale's typical materials are combined. The blending is skillful, with little direct moral exhortation, with barely a trace of reproof to his listeners, but with a constant assurance, based upon common sense as firmly as on biblical texts, that any man who tries can perform God's work better than he does. Hale's examples in support of this cheerful prediction are drawn from his wide reading as often as from his experience as a minister. Thus the sermon "God is a Spirit" is definition by examples from the Bible, Greek myth, and cultural history—Copernicus and Newton. In "The Men of Gadara," a warning against complacency, the substance is biblical, with modern parallels. In the Christmas sermon "Christ the Giver," the material is historical; Hale contrasts the Roman "heyday" of lust and wretchedness with the accomplishments and promise of church growth; and he illustrates the contrast largely by a paradoxical analysis of Edward Gibbon's skeptical comments on the early church. As skillful a combination as any is the sermon "The Possible Boston" in which the church history of the city forms the basis for an appeal for continued expansion of the church's social services.

Other collections, *From Thanksgiving to Fast* (1878) and *The Life in Common* (1880), develop the same subjects. Although Hale has frequently been called a "social gospeler"—which he unquestionably was in part[9]—his own favorite designations for his inclination or predilection were "Liberal Protestant Minister," "Unitarian Christian Minister," or simply "Christian Minister." Clearly aware as he was of social problems, his interests were broad; and he addressed himself to his auditors, Sunday after Sunday, as, first and foremost, individuals responsible for their conduct—for their private lives no less than their public responsibilities. In this sense, Hale was no more an exponent of *the* social gospel, exclusively, than of mysticism or of "muscular Christianity."[10]

Hale's son and biographer, writing a few years after his father's death and thirty-five years after these publications, looked back with particular nostalgia to his father's sermons from this period around 1880. In print, they remain alive and pertinent after nearly a hundred years; they also show that his thinking matured, that his personality was fully formed, and that his expression was completely under control.

III *Later Sermons and Prayers, 1886–1904*

Several years after the discontinuance of weekly publication, three additional collections of Hale's sermons were published. They show little change in either design or substance from his earlier sermons. His presence in the pulpit became more venerable and august as he approached and passed seventy, but the printed versions for his larger congregation away from home carried much the same familiar messages. He noted this himself in 1892, on the fiftieth anniversary of his first boyhood sermons in Massachusetts. Referring to his manuscripts, "somewhat yellow from time," he reread them with an almost impersonal interest, pleased that his first texts had celebrated love: "That perfect love casts out fear, and that this love must show itself in action and not in word,—this may be said to be a fair foundation for whatever the pulpit has to say or do."[11]

Readers who find cosmic optimism cloying should note that Hale's comments on contemporaries are not invariably commendatory. He can find nothing lovable in the "wretched and worthless life of Mr. [Jay] Gould" (*Sermons of the Winter*, 114) and little justification for two heresy trials being conducted by the Presbyterian Church. Such words as *religiosity, ecclesiasticism,* and "stupid idolatry"(17), along with "creed-bound sects"(42), *literalists,* and *word-worshippers,* express an exasperation not nearly so evident a half-century or a quarter-century before. Hale's faith needed no support from *magic tricks,* as he called them; and he was shocked that individual doctrinaires, sentimentalists, and ritualists could still debate how deep the water had been when John baptized Jesus in the Jordan, while society suffered from urbanization with its poverty, crime, drunkenness, lust, and beggary—the hell that Hale exhorted his congregation to obliterate.

In May 1899, Hale informed his church that he would retire later in the year. As he knew, at seventy-seven he was no longer meeting the responsibilities of an active minister. A distinguished successor was appointed, a Harvard professor and the father of an even more distinguished personality, a boy born in 1894, the poet E. E. Cummings. Though Hale had no intention of complete retirement—for he continued lecturing and writing—he could have had no premonition of the honor that would persuade him to resume his ministerial work in 1904 as chaplain of the Senate of the United States. Hale was understandably gratified by his election to the position, late in 1903, by unanimous vote of the senators. The reason he gave for his selection—namely, that he was the oldest candidate—was not the only one, as he well knew.

The celebrated anecdote of Hale's chaplaincy, expertly told by Van Wyck Brooks, is not so unambiguous as it appears. According to the story, Hale was asked if he prayed for the senators; and he is supposed to have answered, "No, Madame, I do not pray for the senators. I look at the senators and pray for the country."[12] There is no reason to doubt the authenticity of Hale's reply, but it should be understood within a framework of respect for the senators as well as concern for the country. He knew every one of them personally and regarded them, as he said in his preface to *Prayers in The Senate* (1904), as "intelligent men, in very close daily intimacy with each other, in the discharge of a common duty of the greatest importance"(vi). That he also regarded them as men in need of instruction, whom he would address as if he were chaplain "in a school or college"(vi), was a privilege of his eighty years plus.

The printed prayers themselves, from the first four months of 1904, are brief extemporaneous statements and restatements in simple language of the fundamental concepts accepted by men of good will. Thus they are virtually a synopsis of Hale's sermons, emphasizing the fatherhood of God and the universal brotherhood of man. Helping others is freedom as well as duty, and "bear ye one another's burdens"(5), one of Hale's favorite texts, means that "we do not pray for ourselves alone"(10). The entire world is every man's concern: "We pray to Thee for this city, for the nation, for the countries everywhere, that they may be knit together in peace"(17).

These are Hale's basic ideals, his message as a minister and as a venerable citizen. In one of their many combinations they become, "Father, we pray for all sorts and conditions of men. . . . [We pray] that the world may be a brighter world and a better world because each of us has lived this day"(111). Among his last words as a Christian minister, they were also among his first—the central message and the goal of his six decades of religious service.

CHAPTER 9

Appraisals

CRITICAL analysis of Edward Everett Hale's writings emphasizes the impression that his most notable accomplishment was the image he created of himself. His assertion that "personal presence rules the world" fits his career to its smallest detail; his personal magnetism, or charisma as it might be called today, was extraordinary. His sincerity and complete unselfishness were obvious to all people who met him, and an important result was that he was a valuable proponent for limited causes like support for a college or preservation of a church. Broader campaigns for social reform, however, necessarily involve committees and team work; whether the immediate outcome is success or failure, the contributions of individuals are usually impossible to assess. Often the value of the project is debatable for years. Municipal ownership of public transportation facilities—for which Hale campaigned actively in the late nineteenth century—is only one example of a cause that is being advocated and opposed no less vigorously a century later.

Hale's contemporaries found inspiration in his idealism. Possibly he never had a strikingly original idea—as compared with a Charles Darwin in Hale's day, or a Sigmund Freud—but he brilliantly represented upper class reformers in their most sincere endeavors to create "a brighter, better world." Progress toward a goal meant more to Hale than the prospect of perfection. He knew that his new civilization could never be achieved; yet temporary expedients like Jane Addams' Hull House "settlement" in Chicago, inadequate as they have become for meeting the later demands for welfare, genuinely sweetened the lives of several generations of ghetto dwellers.

The more widely Hale tried to popularize his projects, the less immediately effective he became. Thus his books, always intelligent, become less vivid when not reinforced by the hypnotic

102

glamour of his presence. "Character is essential" to a successful life, Hale declared; his books retain character because of the graceful literary style, but the ideas hover on the edge of platitude. The nation might indeed be the better and brighter for reexamining Hale's moral statements, translating them into appropriate terms for today. They are applicable, but no more novel than the simple biblical texts from which Hale paraphrased them.

I *Indulgent Reviewers*

For a writer whose vogue was as temporary as Hale's, the comments of his first readers and reviewers are a valuable record of the hold he had on his public. "Everyone knows that Mr. Hale is the prince of story tellers," one admiring journalist wrote. Another writer, who unconsciously revealed his doubt, rashly asserted, "it is unanimously conceded that Mr. Hale has no superior in this country as a writer of short stories." With more assurance, others announced that "no American writer of fiction is more highly appreciated," that "he has hardly his equal as a writer of short stories," and that "critics delight to honor the purity and grace of his style."[1] That these tributes, and a dozen more like them, could have been assembled in 1884 to advertize two of his lesser works is difficult for a twentieth century reader-critic to accept.

Like other authors, Hale was of two minds about reviews of his books: he prized them or despised them emotionally rather than rationally, and he did so in proportion to the critic's understanding and approval of his purposes. His publishers, whose reactions were less complicated, circulated only the favorable notices of a book in the hope of stimulating sales of its successors. In fact, Roberts Brothers, Hale's publishers for many years, made full use of their opportunity to spread the good word of favorable reader responses. Without difficulty they collected commendations from twenty sources, some of which they repeated year after year into the 1890s, as long as the firm remained in business. His other publishers— Cassell, and Lothrop—followed the same practice. Even the more dignified Macmillan Company fell into line in *Tarry at Home Travels,* Hale's last book, with a page of praise from five reviewers for *Memories of a Hundred Years,* but with not a hint of adverse comments or reservations by an equal number of equally well-qualified critics.

The reviews thus quoted serve several purposes today. Primarily they show the kind of admiration felt by Hale's public, the support given him by his publishers, and the social and intellectual qualities of his readers. Inevitably the favorable verdicts are quoted from the Boston papers—the *Globe*, the *Home Journal*, the *Post*, the *Transcript*, and his former family property, the *Advertiser;* from the religious press—the *National Baptist*, the *Congregationalist*, the *New Church Magazine*, the *Presbyterian*, the *Universalist Quarterly*, among others; and from small communities—the Albany *Journal*, the Buffalo *Commercial*, the Louisville *Daily Ledger*, and the San Francisco *Chronicle*. A few laudatory comments were culled from New York papers—the *Commercial Advertiser*, the *Tribune*, and the *Times*. Professional ethics restrained Roberts Brothers from appropriating adaptable quotable phrases from the *Atlantic Monthly*—ones that began with William Dean Howells' notes on Hale's first collections of stories—because they were published by a rival firm.[2]

On the whole, Hale was justified in his retrospective verdict about his reviewers, that he "hardly ever had any ill-natured critics," though he was slightly forgetful in adding that "I am sure I should not have cared if I had" *(Works*, X, x). At the beginning of his career, the *North American Review* greeted his *Kanzas and Nebraska* as "remarkably full and satisfactory" and *Ninety Days' Worth of Europe* as "an individual but not narrow view" marked by "intelligent appreciation".[3] A half-century later the *Dial* was writing in the same vein, praising a new edition of *How To Live* for "well known practical sense and felicity of phrasing" and finding *Memories of a Hundred Years*, in a long and enthusiastic review, a "feast" of anecdotes and "valuable reminiscences."[4] The *American Historical Review* also commended this book, in spite of its "lapses" and "prejudices," as "highly entertaining," with "delightful personality" and a "vivacious and natural style."[5] A few years later the New York *Times* of December 1, 1906, like the *Atlantic Monthly* and the *Review of Reviews*, found *Tarry at Home Travels* more stimulating than most books of travel.[6]

For fifty years following "My Double and How He Undid Me," cleverness was an attribute unfailingly assigned Hale. As Lowell wrote to his editorial successor James T. Fields on November 30, 1863, he had read *The Man Without a Country* with "singular pleasure"; and he described it as "the cleverest story in the *Atlantic* since 'My Double' (also his), which appeared in *my* time." Lowell added the advice to "get more of him" as "he has that lightness of touch and ease of narration that are worth everything."[7] But cleverness was not enough to grant Hale for, as one journalist noted, "The word *clever*, even in the superlative degree, describes only one side of his character." Hale was also sensible; "his pages are crowded with good sense and practical wisdom." This combination was also praised by the Boston *Transcript* in *The Ingham Papers:* "They are not written simply to amuse, but have a graver purpose."

The combination of liveliness and instruction was as frequently noted as the cleverness and the good sense complex. "Delightful as well as instructive" became a standard description of almost everything Hale wrote, whether fiction, exhortation, or, occasionally, sermons. The statement "full of sparkle, quaint humor, and right sentiment," a felicitous grouping of traits well recognized, is paralleled by "the beauty and purity of its sentiments, as well as the bright interest of the story." According to his publisher's blurb, a book by Hale would be "full of humor, pathos, and instruction," a prediction with which reviewers agreed; they found it "bewitching" with a "merry ring," or, at a higher pitch of enthusiasm, "unflagging entertainment, helpfulness, suggestive practical hints, and a contagious vitality that sets one's blood tingling." Critics united in declaring that Hale wrote "racily and earnestly," that he was "read with interest by all classes," and that his books were sensible, practical, and would do "anybody" good to read.

Hale was recognized, except in those stories where he was being deliberately preposterous, as a Realist, because of the "thorough naturalness" of his language, because of the accuracy of his settings, because of the soundness of his sentiments. Thus the reviewer in *Town Topics* could find in Hale's *Sybil Knox* his "characteristic realisms of American thought, life, and language." In the same vein, the *New Church Magazine* wraps up a neat package in praise of *Ups and Downs:* "It delineates American life so graphically that we feel as if Mr. Hale must have seen every rood of ground he describes, and must have known personally every character he so cleverly depicts."

Historically, Hale was also regarded as a Realist, less for *Philip Nolan's Friends* than for *East and West* which, according to the *Ohio State Journal*, "depicts pioneer life in Ohio so as to throw around it an interest never excelled, and perhaps never equalled." *The Churchman* suggested the basis of the public feeling for Hale's

Realism because he was "a man who, almost from his first youth, was in touch with the currents of national life and in deep sympathy with the deeper impulses of the national spirit."

Reviewers recognized the independence of Hale's thought and the individuality of expression that contributed to what they felt was his unconventional personality. The quality of uniqueness is frequently implied in their comments, but the word itself is at times used. "If one desires something unique," an unidentified person wrote of *Crusoe in New York*, "full of wit, a veiled sarcasm that is rich in the extreme, it will all be found in this charming little book." One review of *His Level Best* expressed admiration for his style, "fresh, frank, pungent, straightforward, and pointed," and another admired the crisp, bright, pleasant flavor of *Gone to Texas*, exhibiting "whatever is lovely in the spirit of its author."

During the 1880s Hale's reputation remained high. Professor Henry A. Beers of Yale praised him in 1887 for "a humor all his own," a compliment that was more specific in *The Critic and New Literature* for January 19, 1884, since it noted a "delicate" quality "which makes it much more than merely funny." "Fresh," "readable," "praiseworthy" were adjectives used by the *Critic* in describing a different book, in 1888; and of still another, from 1885: "his sprightliness would make the dullest subject interesting if he cared to take hold of it."[8]

Howells's comments on *Mr. Tangier's Vacations* and *My Friend the Boss*, which Hale had sent him in 1888, never reached print; but Howells' personal letter of thanks to Hale is in the same vein—a measure of praise for both intention and execution, but more particularly admiration for Hale's unique combination of earnestness and charm.[9]

As noted earlier, Hale endured most negative criticism nonchalantly. He never ceased being amused by an early humorless complaint about "My Double and How He Undid Me" that it was *improbable*. "I think it is," he agreed, "but I think the moral important." To discount the chronic antagonism of the austere *Nation*, he devised the rationalization that its original editor, E. L. Godkin, an immigrant from Britain, never understood the realities of life in the United States. On meeting Godkin, Hale was surprised when he "proved to be an agreeable person"; and he was again surprised a few years later when Godkin "most cordially" asked him to contribute to the magazine—an invitation that he managed to decline.[10]

Hale's hold on public esteem during his heyday is illustrated by a survey article of April 12, 1884, in the *Critic and Good Literature*, then the leading magazine of its type. The article resulted from a poll undertaken by the magazine to select the members of an American academy to be modeled on the French institution. Three hundred writers were nominated; the most popular received one hundred and thirty votes; the least popular, a paragraph of names alphabetically arranged, with from ten to one votes, included Paul Hayne, Robert Ingersoll, William James, S. Weir Mitchell, Henry W. Shaw (Josh Billings), Frank R. Stockton, Lew Wallace, and the still anonymous author of *The Breadwinners*.

Among the forty leaders in this race for immortality Edward Everett Hale ranked eleventh with an even one hundred votes. Among those above him, he would have unhesitatingly deferred to the top men, Holmes(130), Lowell(128), Whittier(125), Bancroft(121), and Howells(119). Below them, however, it is difficult to admit the superior worthiness of George William Curtis (118 votes), Thomas Bailey Aldrich(111), Francis Bret Harte(105), Edmund Clarence Stedman(104), or Richard Grant White(102). Hale's chances of being remembered were, and are, as good as theirs. The readers of the *Critic and Good Literature* were not endowed with noteworthy powers of discernment: Henry James was thirteenth among their choices, Mark Twain was fourteenth, and Walt Whitman was twentieth. Francis Parkman, number forty, received fewer than half as many votes as Charles Dudley Warner, Henry Ward Beecher, or Richard Henry Stoddard. Herman Melville received no votes.

Success or failure in the *Critic* poll made little difference to history, for the project of forming an academy failed, as had an earlier one from 1868. By 1904, when the present Academy of Arts and Letters was founded, the eligible living writers—deprived by death of such undoubted stars as Holmes, Lowell, Whittier, Whitman—were a different group, hardly more memorable. Yet of the *Critic's* forty, ten were elected to membership in the new Academy; and Hale was among them.

II *The Man in Life*

During Hale's lifetime, the vast majority of recorded appraisals of his personality and character were laudatory. His reputation as a man equaled the respect of reviewers for his writings, and with more reason. He was a man whom it was hard to dislike, and he could not be dismissed either physically or morally as *little*—a mildly disparaging word favored in descriptions of his books. In fact, disparaging appraisals were few and inconclusive. One of his future parishioners at Worcester, disappointed in Hale's first sermon there in 1843, flatly declared, "He has got a splendid voice, and that is all he has got." A more discerning listener protested immediately, "You are rather severe; he has considerable talent [as a young minister], at least great cultivation of mind." A third, who had enjoyed hearing the identical sermon, added that "he shows promise of a great deal of talent, though no genius" (*Life and Letters*, I, 150–51).[11] In later years a number of his friends felt that his sermons were sometimes carelessly or hastily prepared, and they may not have been mistaken. That the sermons were often "flimsy," as John T. Trowbridge asserted of one that he heard about 1853,[12] is refuted by the two hundred in print or by the fifteen hundred in manuscript.

One of the strangest comments critical of Hale's personality was reported by Trowbridge as coming from Moses D. Phillips, the publisher, a close friend of Hale during his early days in Worcester. "Mr. Hale is a very able man," Phillips is supposed to have said, "but I doubt if he ever makes his mark in the world, for the reason that he lacks industry." As Trowbridge, and no doubt Phillips, recognized later, a more faulty diagnosis could hardly have been imagined for a person who established himself not long after as "the greatest worker in Boston" or, as paraphrased by a less than complete admirer, as "Edward Everything Hale."[13]

When Barrett Wendell, visiting Harvard in 1888 for interviews preparatory to joining the faculty, found most of the persons he encountered mediocre or uninteresting, he made an exception of Hale, whose weakness was an "hereditary" hostility to "everything south of New England."[14] Bliss Perry, who was also a new resident of Boston when he came as editor of the *Atlantic*, described Hale about 1900 as "the most picturesque figure" among older members of the Examiner Club, "and the carelessness of his dress was matched by the reckless inaccuracy and vigor of his talk."[15] This charge of reckless or inadvertent inaccuracy in his writing as in his conversation, which can be discounted as almost a cliché reaction to Hale at eighty, cannot be ignored. Senator George F. Hoar, a disciple for whom Hale could do no wrong, yet also a president of the

American Historical Association (in 1895), admitted the existence of incidental mistakes with the explanation that Hale was too busy a man "to verify every unsubstantial detail before he speaks or writes." Hoar loyally maintained that "I do not believe we have a more trustworthy historian than Dr. Hale, as far as giving us the motive and pith and essence of great transactions."[16]

Comments about Hale's careless dress, which is abundantly documented, are sometimes intended less as a criticism than an endearment; for, he was, as Hamilton Wright Mabie surmised, "a figure which Rembrandt would have rejoiced to paint."[17] In his later years how he looked sometimes created more comment than what he said. His heavy beard, giving a permanently unkempt appearance, was due, his son has explained, to his refusal to waste time on shaving and barbering.

After 1870, the year in which the four lend-a-hand mottoes originated, Hale was immune to common criticism, a man incapable of wrongdoing, if not above the errors of judgment inseparable from the human condition. A "minister of the people," an admirer from 1889 exclaimed, "may he long continue as such, for the people need him!"[18] The transformation of Hale from a literary and ethical man into a public figure, virtually complete during the last decade of his life, owed much to his association with Theodore Roosevelt, which had begun many years back during Roosevelt's undergraduate days at Harvard (1876–1880) when Hale was one of the overseers and a campus religious leader. The two were fraternity brothers in Alpha Delta Phi, a literary club in Hale's undergraduate years that had later been suppressed with other secret societies and revived in 1879 under Hale's leadership. Roosevelt, then a junior, was one of the students who gave Hale major assistance. The restoration of the club's legality was celebrated publicly in a meeting at which Hale presided and at which the young Roosevelt spoke, "the first speech I ever made," he recalled, "one whose extreme badness was only relieved by its brevity."[19]

Although Roosevelt could not attend the public celebration of Hale's eightieth birthday in Symphony Hall, Boston, he sent a graceful eulogistic note to be read by Senator Hoar, the principal speaker. Like Timoleon at Syracuse, said President Roosevelt—who had received more education in the Classics than most of his successors in that office—Hale belonged among "the noblest and most attractive figures in all history." At the Harvard commencement of the same year, Roosevelt placed a medal of honor around Hale's neck at the Alpha Delta Phi testimonial. "Of course I was brought up on your books, sir," he said. "I should be wholly unable to explain the debt I owe you not only for the particular influence you wrought, but for the whole spirit that went through all your writings."[20]

Roosevelt, a great politician as well as a loyal alumnus, was able to use Hale's immunity to criticism in furthering the election of William Howard Taft in 1908. Several letters on the subject are reprinted in the sixth volume of Roosevelt's correspondence. One of these (Oyster Bay, August 28, 1908) to "Dear Will," expresses indignation at the "nonsensical" attacks on Taft's Unitarianism, and suggests mentioning that Chaplain Hale of the Senate is also a Unitarian, and that there is not "in all the United States a man more revered by the clergymen of every denomination, a man with whom every true Christian must feel eager to be associated in Christian brotherhood." In another letter (October 16, 1908), Hale is to Roosevelt "one of the most revered men in or out of the ministry in all the United States," and in a third letter (November 6, 1908) he is "an American of whose life all good Americans are proud."[21]

With this kind of backing Hale's position was secure. In 1906, shortly before the death of Susan B. Anthony, the suffragette leader, a Chicago editor asked, "Is she not clearly the foremost citizen in the United States today, man or woman?" Hedging a bit, the Reverend Jenkyn Lloyd Jones added, "We dare say this with no disrespect to President Roosevelt or to Edward Everett Hale, the next in line of honored citizens."[22] Earlier in the twentieth century, a well-informed, enthusiastic appraisal in the *Review of Reviews* had summarized Hale's reputation as "Boston's leading citizen for many years, and one of the greatest—some would say, the greatest—of living Americans."[23] In reckless admiration, another writer claimed for Hale "planetary influence" through the "broad humanity" of his writings and his "spurring spirit of an intense moral enthusiasm," his "intense patriotism," and his other qualities that in combination sum up to "his merited distinction as a great American."[24]

"Dr. Hale has done a good many things in his own matchless fashion," Senator Hoar declared at Hale's eightieth birthday celebration; and he listed a dozen accomplishments as diverse as writing *The Man Without a Country*, organizing the Lend-a-Hand clubs, and "devis[ing] the plan that might have saved Texas from slavery, and thereby prevented the Civil War."[25] Less questionably, "Edward Everett Hale has been the interpreter of a pure, simple loving and living faith to thousands and thousands of souls."[26] After more of the same emotional eulogy, between the inevitable references to Daniel Defoe and Abou Ben Adhem, came Hoar's oratorical climax: "He has pictured for us the infinite desolation of the man without a country. But when his time shall come, what will be the desolation of the country without the man!"[27]

The press obituary notices about Hale's death in 1909 went, and could go, no farther in praising his accomplishments. The Associated Press sent out a full column obituary from Boston, a shorter story from its Washington office, and statements by notables wherever they were found. Among these was Mark Twain, located in Baltimore, who was quoted as saying, "I had the greatest esteem and respect for Dr. Hale, and the greatest admiration for his work." Various pictures of Hale in old age were used, and the obituary from Boston was run as front page news by papers as distant as the Los Angeles *Times* (June 11), which added a highly emotional combination of headlines: "Grand Old Man . . . Long, Noble Life of Toil is Ended . . . Nation Mourns His Death."

The weekly and monthly magazines paid their respects in the same terms that the newspapers had used. The *Outlook,* always favorable to Hale as a star contributor, printed four articles in June 1909: an editorial, an analysis by Thomas Wentworth Higginson, brief tributes from President Taft and Henry Cabot Lodge, and a reprint of *The Man Without a Country* with an editorial endorsement. The *Review of Reviews* offered cordial estimates and Albert Shaw's penetrating observation: "a more truly national personage, in his knowledge and sympathies, than were any of the other New England thinkers and leaders."[28] Even the *Nation* obituary was respectful, though not eulogistic. "Early in his ministry he took a high rank in the Unitarian fellowship," the writer granted, with the addition of concrete details describing Hale's preaching: "His presence was commanding; his gutteral voice extremely powerful and impressive, with a wide range from the most gentle to the harshest notes; his sermons ethical in their substance and vivid in their style." Among his writings *Ten Times One Is Ten* and *In His Name* were mentioned as the "most widely read" of his longer narratives and "The Man Without a Country" as "probably the most popular short story written in America."[29]

III *Coda*

Hale's preeminence as a public figure could not be expected to outlive him, but his memory was cherished by his friends. Thus John Burroughs, looking at Bela Pratt's statue of Hale in 1913, recalled him as "a very lovable character" with a "great fund of humanity" and "very ready sympathy," a man "to sweeten life and keep it sane and wholesome."[30] Another friend of many years, Lilian Whiting, writing in 1918 and recalling Hale's "unique and vigorous personality" and "the spiritual vitality that he radiated," was not surprised that his former church was "habitually" referred to by his name as "Dr. Hale's church." He was, she reported, "a spiritual dynamo," the "patron saint of every conceivable enterprise," with "a singular gift of galvanizing other people into work."[31]

To Lyman Abbott, compiling *Silhouettes of My Contemporaries* in 1921, Hale remained "an American Abou Ben Adhem." A greater compliment paid him was that of Charles W. Eliot who, when speaking extemporaneously at his ninetieth birthday celebration in 1924, stated: "I do not know any better advice to give to the graduates of Harvard College, or to the undergraduates, than that contained in those two phrases of Edward Everett Hale's: 'Look forward and not backward—look out and not in.' "[32]

Another Harvard colleague from the past, Francis Greenwood Peabody, wrote in the same vein and with greater detail in a study of Hale's personality in his *Reminiscences of Present-Day Saints* (1927), the last and best treatment of this subject. In brief, he knew Hale as a "rare and generous genius" who was greatly loved, his "special characteristic" or gift being "the extraordinary lavishness of his affection, the prodigality of his sympathy".[33]

In comparison with such tributes from friends and colleagues, recipients of Hale's generosity and counsel, the continued acceptance of his writings was meager indeed. It is not surprising that an old friend like M. A. DeWolfe Howe should have referred optimistically but questionably as a judgment to *The Man Without a Country* in 1919 as a "national classic" seemingly assured, "by universal consent, of a permanent place in literature."[34] It is astonishing, however, to read in a 1950 treatise on historical novels that *Philip Nolan's Friends* is "authentic"—the accompanying "urbane" might be tolerated—or in a scholarly history of American fiction completed in 1936 that it is a "novelette."[35] Fred Lewis Pattee's brief discus-

sion in his *Development of the American Short Story* (1923), though
limited to some few of Hale's early writings, is accurate in recognizing his "remarkable" youthful stories in the *Boston Miscellany* and
his discovery of the "Marjorie Daw" or O. Henry type of surprise
ending "years before the Civil War." Hale stood for Realism of a
sort, Pattee noted, "what might be called realistic extravagance," an
extravagance not wholly unrestrained fantasy, but a kind of "ex-
travaganza touched with specific realism"(183–85).[36]

Hale's hold on the memory of men too young to have known him
in life is due in large part to the effective statue by Bela Lyon Pratt
that was unveiled on Boston Common in 1913. The sculptor, who
was New England born and who had lived in Boston since 1893, had
ample opportunity to observe his subject as he appeared at the
beginning of the new century. Hale survives in Pratt's statue as in
life, bearded, slightly stooped, covered by a great coat, holding a
walking stick in one hand and a wide-brimmed hat in the other. As
he stands in the midst of handsome gardens, writes a recent observer, he is looking southwest across the pond with tired eyes and a
passive, noncommittal expression.

Gamaliel Bradford, writing in 1920 shortly after the success of his
Damaged Souls, was less impressed. Although Bradford had known
Hale and was thoroughly aware of his reputation, he admitted his
own failure to appreciate the central core or to get a clear focus on
Hale's personality. According to his journal and letters Bradford,
who had been tempted to make a psychographic analysis of Hale,
gave up in despair. This renunciation was not unique, for Bradford
gave up also, at about the same time, on Peter Lesley, a minister
before becoming a geologist, and Phillips Brooks, an Episcopalian
bishop and orator of the first rank. Although Bradford blamed himself as possibly prejudiced against the ministerial profession, he
found the three of them verbose and empty. He complained to M.
A. DeWolfe Howe of Hale's "utter barrenness" and he wrote to
Robert Frost about a "vast flood of verbal sanctity" in which souls
like Hale's "seemed to have quite evaporated." Why, he wondered,
should he enjoy a rascal like Aaron Burr, and reject a saint?[37]

William James, who also knew Hale, must have suffered nearly as
acutely twenty years earlier while writing *Varieties of Religious Experience* (1902), although he achieved a tactful fusion of compliment
and apprehension when he praised Hale as an expression of the
"once-born" type of religious consciousness "with no element of

morbid compunction or crisis." With this statement, James coupled his misgiving about a cheerful temperament "fatally forbidden to linger . . . over the darker aspects of the universe" as an optimism capable of becoming "quasi-pathological" or "a kind of congenital anesthesia." Hale himself, he concluded, represents "healthy-mindedness" which, like "an inability to feel evil," he rated as only one of "the simpler kinds of religious happiness."[38] This reservation is almost as devastating as Gamaliel Bradford's more vivid phrases—not intended for publication—about Hale as "a reek and mist of words" that were seemingly intelligent, colorful, impassioned, earnest: "Yet when you examine them and meditate upon them, there is somehow—nothing there. . . ."[39] Nothing, that is, for the psychographer's purpose.

Hale's reputation as a man of letters evaporated with the emergence of the "new" literature at about the time of World War I. He was overwhelmed by stereotypes of rejection—the genteel tradition; American Victorianism; Indian Summer—from which only the nonconformists escaped. Even Howells and James suffered, and the few survivors were Melville, who had been forgotten; Emily Dickinson, who had been unpublished; Henry Adams, who had been rebellious; or William De Forest, who had been overlooked. What could Hale say in the 1920s to the self-christened lost generation or the self-righteous Babbitts of the boom years? He simply did not belong in the world of Henry Ford and Taylorism, James Joyce and Freudian psychoanalysis. Not even the possibility of regarding him as a *Socialist*—to stretch the point a bit—availed against the necessary qualifying adjective *Christian*.

After the failure of the war to end war by making the world safe for democracy, *The Man Without a Country*, known for years as a document on Americanism on the level of George Washington's Farewell Address and Daniel Webster's Bunker Hill oration, was threatened with disgrace and rejection as an apology for imperialism. This charge against Hale does not die: as late as 1965 a historian described a sermon by Hale in 1862 (April 13) as "provincial pride" in a hoped-for Northern victory that would bring the South a New England "civilization" with its "church and schoolhouse," its "forge and factory," a formula that the historian interpreted as "imperialist exploitation under the guise of Yankee benevolence."[40]

The temptation is almost irresistible to reprove Hale for having scattered his talents; yet if he had not been, on principle, jack of all trades, he might still have been master of none. To his credit, he was resolved not to do things that he disapproved. Yet this determination exposed him to criticism. He avoided theological debate—therefore, he was accused of being unintellectual. He scolded neither God nor man—therefore, his religious convictions were said to be shallow. In expression, he avoided purple patches, preferring conversational language—therefore, he was suspected of being emotionally undeveloped or esthetically insensitive. He never modified his complete faith in a benevolent God—therefore, he was patronized as naive.

Prophecy is a risky occupation. An enthusiastic writer in the New York *Times* (January 7, 1899) foresaw a long life for Hale's writings. Rereading the humorous stories and remembering *Our New Crusade* as "the most sensible temperance tract ever published in this land," he concluded with a prediction: "Possibly, when all Americans are as sensible as the Sybarites and as patriotic as Philip Nolan learned to be they will find nothing novel in the volumes [of Hale's *Works*], but that will not happen tomorrow."[41] The *Dial*, nearer the mark, noted that Hale was a voice "from a day more remote in feeling than in time."[42]

Though it is hard to foresee a revival of Hale as a popular author, there are good reasons for students and scholars to remember him.[43] A mirror of his period, he reflects some events not caught so clearly by others. Often entertaining, he is more significant as an educator and as a journalist than as a creative writer; he is always the promoter and protagonist, the middleman of ideas that are hardly original in themselves but that are fruitful for social improvement.

The majority of causes that Hale advocated in his new civilization were progressive. Long before President Franklin Roosevelt specified the Four Freedoms in 1941—freedom of expression, freedom of worship, freedom from want, freedom from fear—Hale had subscribed wholeheartedly to them and a few more. President John F. Kennedy would have revealed nothing new to Hale in his inaugural plea to place country above self; for this placement, which had been a central doctrine of Hale many years before Kennedy's birth, was no more than an invigorating restatement of a Harvard rule of conduct to which Hale had significantly contributed.

More specifically, Hale realized the seriousness of urban pathology and wrote repeatedly for slum clearance, rapid transit, and better treatment for the Negro minority. For the nation as well, he pleaded sensibly for raising the standard of living, enriching public education, and conserving natural resources. He advocated public ownership of utilities and government regulation of monopolies. He enthusiastically welcomed the progress of technology and looked upon the settlement of the Middle and Far West as an extension of Americanism. On these subjects, among many others, his words remain worthy of attention.

For a man who took a stand on many issues, Hale has a good record for being so often on what was shown to be the better side. Occasionally he used poor judgment, as most will agree, in his old-fashioned skepticism about woman suffrage and in his antagonism toward labor unions. On other issues, such as a military draft or the control of dangerous drugs and the regulation of pornographic literature, the tactics he advocated are not pertinent today and are difficult to acquit of ambiguity or contradiction at the time. His opposition to a military draft rested on his opinion that volunteers fight better. He favored freedom of the press, but it is embarrassing to an admirer to find him named as an officer of the New England Society for the Suppression of Vice, later the Watch and Ward Society, and to be reminded that he was one of the prominent citizens who welcomed Anthony Comstock to Boston.[44] Yet Hale was not a prude, for no prude could have admired Benjamin Franklin so highly or have greeted *Leaves of Grass* so warmly. Neither a misogynist nor a labor baiter, he was a man of independent judgment for which, fortunately, he did not claim infallibility.

As Gamaliel Bradford discovered, Hale's accomplishments are impossible to dramatize. His activities were so varied that they do not shape up as a formula for a cultural portrait. His place in many movements is as minor as in the history of photography, but significant enough for him to be remembered, at least in a footnote, as "the most distinguished of the Bostonians to try his hand at daguerreotypy" as early as 1839.[45] He was equally proud of having been a short-term geologist in his youth and pleased at having a peak in the White Mountains named Mount Hale as recognition for his successful campaign for reforestation. His writing helped in the overthrow of the Louisiana lottery, and he contributed to the development of neighborhood settlement houses and associated charities.[46] These involvements were among his footnote achievements, but they are a par with his pioneer advocacy of Latin American and Spanish studies, his correction of the map of the Isle of Brazil, his knowledge of roses, and his research on the air "Yankee Doodle."[47]

Hale was known as reformer and philanthropist, terms which, applied in the meanings he accepted, were compliments. More fundamentally, he was always an educator. His teaching took at least three forms: (1) through the example of his own conduct; (2) through his writings of fiction, biography, history, presenting real or imagined examples; and (3) by direct exhortation, as in his books of advice and some of his sermons. The type of education he espoused had several goals, but the most elementary of them was the direct diffusion of knowledge. Too important to be restricted to schools and colleges, the spreading of information was also to be accomplished on the open market by newspapers and magazines; by lyceum lectures and public meetings; and through fiction, poetry, and drama. Such diffusion of knowledge should be accompanied by the encouragement of curiosity about the entire created universe; by the development of attitudes and ideals; and eventually by the stimulation of activities aiming at social betterment.

Like other teachers, Hale was primarily a transmitter of cultural values. In his writing he was neither complete artist nor scholar; he was a little of both. As an individual, he was one of the most likeable men of his time, a model of good citizenship; and thousands of persons thought of him as *great*.

Notes and References

Chapter One

1. Dates and names are taken, except as noted, from the standard biography, *The Life and Letters of Edward Everett Hale* by his son, E. E. Hale, Jr. (Boston, 1917).

2. This letter from Edward Everett Hale to his brother Charles appears in part in *Life and Letters*, I, 384–90.

3. Throughout my discussion, quotations from Hale's books are usually from their first editions, as listed in my bibliography. The "Library Edition" of Hale's *Works*, in ten volumes (New York, 1898–1900), has also been used (as for *A New England Boyhood*); but this set contains only a small part of his writings.

4. Willard Thorpe notes that Hale in his travel books showed "extraordinary openmindedness" toward esthetics; he taught himself to enjoy Romanesque and Byzantine art and primitive painting, none of which were included in the approved canon of his time and class *(Literary History of the United States* [New York, 1948], p. 830). The same openmindedness, it should be added, is part of Hale's view of life and one of his most attractive characteristics. Though unmistakably WASP—White Anglo-Saxon Protestant—he was not rigid in his prejudices, which were more often residues from the past than consciously held and advocated principles.

5. Page references to *Memories of a Hundred Years* are to the second edition, revised and with three additional chapters (New York, 1904).

6. More than seventy volumes of Hale's diaries, starting in 1834, are preserved in the huge Hale collection in the New York State Library in Albany. With them are early family writings (imitation newspapers, a continuation of *Swiss Family Robinson*, an unpublished romance "The Belle of Belleville") and school and college class exercises, translations, and compositions.

7. Hale had lectured semiseriously on this subject at the Lowell Institute and elsewhere, and he also wrote a report for the American Antiquarian Society *Proceedings* (XV, new series [1902], 98–102).

Chapter Two

1. Van Wyck Brooks, *New England: Indian Summer* (New York, 1940), p. 418.

2. The genealogy appeared as Appendix A, pp. 185–202, of I. W. Stuart, *Life of Captain Nathan Hale, the Martyr-Spy of the American Revolution* (Hartford, Conn., 1856).

3. Most of the tributes referred to are listed in Jean Holloway's excellent bibliography in *Bulletin of Bibliography*, XXI (1954–55), 89–92, 114–20, 140–43.

4. During the post–Civil War reconstruction years, Hale could not share Lowell's belief that (as Hale summarized it) "a new wave of Philistinism had overwhelmed the administration of America." Hale commented tersely, "I think he was wrong"(211), and added a paragraph of apology that can be explained only as a victory of Hale's optimism over his passion for reform.

5. A charming supplement to Hale's book is his preface to a collection of Lowell's *Early Prose Writings* published by John Lane (New York, 1902).

6. Hale's negative reports are quoted in *Life and Letters*, I, 122–23, and alluded to in *Works*, VIII, 290. Letters from Emerson to Hale are reprinted in Ralph L. Rusk's edition of Emerson's *Letters* (New York, 1939), IV, 134–35, dated March 17, 1849; *ibid.*, 532, October 8, 1855; and VI, 99, January 26, 1870.

7. M. A. DeWolfe Howe, *Memories of a Hostess* (Boston, 1922), p. 93.

8. Hale's formal tribute in *Works*, vol. VIII, is eulogistic without reservation. See also Emerson's *Two Unpublished Essays* (Boston, 1896) with Hale's six page introduction of restrained praise for these "curious and valuable" undergraduate papers.

9. Laura E. Richards and Maude Howe Elliott, *Julia Ward Howe 1819–1910* (Boston, 1916), II, 268, 272–73.

10. Howard N. Meyer, *Colonel of the Black Regiment* (New York, 1967), 49. The complete study of Higginson is Tilden G. Edelstein's *Strange Enthusiasm; A Life of Thomas Wentworth Higginson* (New Haven, Conn., 1968).

11. The main collection of Hale manuscripts at the New York State Library in Albany has been used expertly by his biographers. Collections in the Huntington Library and the Massachusetts Historical Society have also been cited in published studies. Many more of his letters have apparently never been examined closely. For access to approximately two thousand of these (which I have referred to without venturing to quote), I am indebted to numerous libraries, including these: American Antiquarian Society; American Philosophical Society; Boston Public Library; Brown University; Charles Patterson Van Pelt Library of the University of Pennsylvania; Columbia University; Haverford College; Houghton Library, Harvard Univer-

sity; Library of Congress; Massachusetts Historical Society; Milton S. Eisenhower Library, Johns Hopkins University; New York Public Library; Pennsylvania Historical Society; Princeton University; Rutherford B. Hayes Library of Fremont, Ohio; University of Rochester; University of Virginia; Yale University. I am furthermore permanently indebted to the invaluable cooperation of my friend and colleague, Dr. William A. Perkins, who sacrificed time during a sabbatical research leave to digest material in libraries that I did not reach personally.

12. Robert Collyer, *Some Memories* (Boston, n. d.; reprinted from *Christian Register*, 1903–04), p. 206.

13. The letter to the *Atlantic* is an James C. Austin's *Fields of the Atlantic Monthly* (San Marino, Calif., 1953), p. 116, a book that includes fourteen letters by Hale. The unpublished letters are held by the New York Public Library; Haverford College; the University of Virginia; and the Houghton Library, Harvard University.

14. Hamlin Garland, *Roadside Meetings* (New York, 1930), pp. 10–11.

15. C. H. Dennis, *Eugene Field's Creative Years* (Garden City, N.Y., 1924), p. 197.

16. Edward P. Mitchell, *Memories of an Editor* (New York, 1924), pp. 74–77. Hale was so indignant about an adverse review of Richard Watson Gilder's first book of poems that he wrote a letter of consolation to the mistreated young author: "It [the harsh notice in the London *Spectator*] made me so angry that I cannot help saying so to you. . . . Pray be sure, dear Mr. Gilder, that it is better to please many readers than it is to write what penny-a-liners cannot find fault with" (Rosamond Gilder, ed., *Letters of Richard Watson Gilder* [Boston, 1916], p. 72).

Chapter Three

1. These references, persuasive propaganda throughout the North when first made, rankled some Southerners for generations. As late as 1899 an orator addressing a group of Confederate veterans attacked Hale's "despicable" slurs upon Bragg, Beauregard, and Maury (without mentioning Vallandigham or Nolan). Embarking on literary criticism, the orator also denounced Hale's "disjointed, infelicitous, and utterly improbable story" as an "inane and commonplace brochure." As a result, the local organization voted to request banning the book from Texas schools. The New York *Times*, speaking editorially on July 25, expressed mild surprise at this belated attack on the "little masterpiece" and at the veterans' confusion between constitutional and literary standards of excellence.

2. Particularly in *Works*, vol. I; and in a "new edition with an introduction in the year of the war with Spain" (Boston, 1898), pp. v–xxii. The only competitor for thoroughness is an unpublished doctoral dissertation by Nancy Esther James, "Realism in Romance: A Critical Study of the Short Stories of Edward Everett Hale" (Pennsylvania State University, 1969). In

two chapters on *The Man Without a Country* (pp. 7–32, 176–200), she examines every facet of the story from its inception in 1863 or earlier to Hale's last words about it. She also presents copious extracts of critical comment from the date of publication to the present and gives ingenious yet plausible comparisons of its mythical or archetypal meanings with legends of the wandering Jew, the flying Dutchman, Homer's Odysseus, Coleridge's ancient mariner, and William Austin's "Peter Rugg, the Missing Man."

3. The rampant discontent and defeatism throughout the North while Hale was writing his story are shown in Wood Gray's *The Hidden Civil War* (New York, 1942), and in Frank L. Klement's *The Copperheads in the Middle West* (Chicago, 1960).

4. Page references are to the first edition of the novel (New York, 1877; copyright 1876).

5. See Noel M. Loomis and Abraham P. Nasatir, *Pedro Vial and the Roads to Santa Fe* (Norman, Okla., 1967), pp. 206–27. In the confused bureaucracy of Spanish Texas, which Hale did not exaggerate, Nolan was the conspiratorial equal of his contemporaries. In both business and love, the historians report, his dealings—devious, sometimes rash—"sowed suspicions that would exist for a long time." The mixture of fact and misdirected imagination in Hale's novel is treated expertly by Jean Holloway in her article "Edward Everett Hale and 'How to Conquer Texas'," in University of Texas *Studies in English*, XXXI (1952), 68–85.

6. "The Real Philip Nolan," Mississippi Historical Society *Proceedings*, IV (1901), 281–329; "Philip Nolan and the Levant," *National Geographic*, XVI (March 1905), 114–16.

7. As required or recommended reading for schools, *The Man Without a Country* has been the subject of numerous "lesson plans" and other teaching devices. Suggestions were published between 1910 and 1940 in the *Elementary English Review*, the *Grade Teacher*, the *Journal of Education*, and the *Normal Instructor*. A few years later it was the subject of a two part discussion in the *English Journal* (XXXVIII [September 1949], 396–97, and XXXIX [March 1950], 163) in which one teacher pointed out the difficulty of persuading high school students that it was not "true" history. The second, in agreement, claimed for it "a psychological and moral truth far more important in literature than historical actuality could be." By intention, it teaches the value of patriotism; but it also suggests to "our generation" the importance of helping "displaced persons" find a welcome in the country to which they have been unwillingly exiled.

8. By William Sloane Kennedy, who is best known as an early champion of Walt Whitman, in a discriminating article, "Edward Everett Hale" in the *Century* (XXIX [January 1885], 338–43). In the same vein, the New York *Times* declared (December 9, 1888) that it "ought to be read over and over again . . . a cleverer fiction with a higher moral never was written."

9. This abusive phrase may have originated with W. P. Garrison in the *Nation*, April 17, 1902. In an unsigned note on a new edition of Hale's story, "in type so bold that it might be thought designed for children," the appeal from reason is added: "Though it has received a fresh certificate of beneficence from President Roosevelt, there are some who look upon it as the primer of Jingoism."

10. During the Liberty Loan drives of World War I, two magazines considered "Take the Loan" relevant enough to merit reprinting: *Outlook* (CXVI [June 13, 1917], 243, and *Woman's Home Companion* (XLIV [November 1917], 2).

11. James D. Hittle, director of national security and foreign affairs for the Veterans of Foreign Wars, in the San Diego *Union*, March 24, 1968. In the same newspaper a civilian stated (September 3, 1965) that of the four things we have to live for—country, family, God, and health—"Our country comes first," as the basis for the others, but that, "if you have never read of 'The Man Without a Country,' then this won't mean much to you." According to editorials in the *Union,* deserters to Sweden will eventually "learn the same lesson as Philip Nolan" (January 13, 1968); but no hope was held out for Eldridge Cleaver, homesick as Philip Nolan but unrepentant (July 22, 1969).

A contributor to the Metropolitan Opera Guild's magazine *Opera News* for February 19, 1972 (XXXVI, 7), has made an odd comparison between Nolan and Ignace Jan Paderewski, the Polish musician and statesman. Unable to learn the exact location of the great pianist's body, "temporarily" resting in Arlington National Cemetery since 1941, Maxine Glassman wrote that "there is an unfortunate flavor of 'The Man Without a Country' about the situation." The U.S. Department of the Army, like the Polish Embassy and delegation to the United Nations, "disclaims knowledge," and "no one seems to know who made the decision."

12. Francis R. Gemme, introduction to *The Man Without a Country and Other Stories*—the others not by Hale—(New York, 1969), pp. 4, 7.

Chapter Four

1. Preface to *Crusoe in New York*, 1880 edition, pp. v–vi.

2. *Ibid.*, p. vi.

3. From *His Level Best*, 1872 edition, pp. 232–33; originally in the *Boston Miscellany of Literature and Fashion*, I (January 1842), 30.

4. Hale's appreciation of Hellenism as extolled by Matthew Arnold was limited and subordinated to a glorification of outgoing Christian benevolence. In his revision of Thomas Bulfinch's *Age of Fable* (Boston, 1882), Hale, unable to eliminate the primitive harshness of the greater myths, admitted his preference for the story of Cupid and Psyche, the latest and gentlest of them all. In a trick story, he used the theme for a modernized version in which a bride loses her husband by learning the secret of his

occupation. In "The Modern Psyche," Mr. E[dward] Ross is a newspaper editor trying to save his home life from business intrusions and obligations. Hale's friend Thomas Wentworth Higginson was sure, however, that as a very young man Hale grasped the Greek spirit superlatively well. He wrote about Hale's "brilliant" translation of Homer's lines on Neptune's descent (in the *Iliad*, book thirteen): "Out of the myriad translations of Homer there is in all English literature but one version known to me of even a single passage which gives in a high degree the Homeric flavor" (*Carlyle's Laugh* [1909], p. 163). The translation, twenty-three lines, is printed in Hale's *Works*, X, 88.

5. From *The Ingham Papers*, 1869 edition, p. 94; first appeared in the *Rosary of Illustrations of the Bible* (1848).

6. From the collection *Susan's Escort* (1897), p. 42; reprinted from the *Independent* (1889). Hale's burlesque of Hawthorne's tale is neither profound nor deeply respectful. Hale did not see it, as later interpreters have, as a study of pride, a negation of Transcendentalism, or an expression of nineteenth century existentialism. (See "The Absurdity of 'The Minister's Black Veil'" by G. A. Santangelo, *Pacific Coast Philology*, V [April 1970], 61–66.) Hale's Reverend Hooper is a practical journeyman minister deliberately misrepresented by an unrealistic storyteller.

7. Such good sense does not guarantee a good story. In "The Rag-Man and the Rag-Woman" (1868), Hale began a satire in which an unemployed insurance agent built a profitable business by saving and selling useless printed material—junk mail, throwaways, and other pollutants. It is moderately amusing until the point is blunted by excessive elaboration.

8. *Susan's Escort*, p. 197.

9. *Stories of Invention, Told by Inventors and Their Friends* (1885), pp. 9–10.

10. Although most readers have liked Hale's Sybaris sketches, beginning with Howells, their first editor (see "Recollections of an Atlantic Editorship" by Howells, *Atlantic Monthly*, C [November 1907], 604), Vernon L. Parrington, Jr., has vigorously expressed a minority view in his *American Dreams: A Study of American Utopias* (New York, 1964; first published in 1947). Hale's views, he said, had no influence on society; Hale was not a serious reformer; he was not a practical man; he was not constructive; and he had no "astuteness," economic or political (pp. 44–47). These are charges that are not without basis when applied to Hale's light fiction (intended for entertainment with moral overtones) but unjustified if applied to Hale's organizing and lobbying for social reforms.

11. In *Our Christmas in a Palace; A Traveller's Story* (1883), pp. 207–26; also in *Works*, vol. IV; originally published in *Harper's* (March 1877).

12. Sam Moskowitz insists on Hale's priority and on the excellence of his story. See his *Explorers of the Infinite: Shapers of Science Fiction* (Cleveland, 1963), pp. 88–98. According to Moskowitz, Hale not only introduced

the sputnik into fiction, but actually conceived the idea of such an invention a quarter century and more before German and Russian claimants. He predicts a probable "peculiar literary immortality" for the story and a fame that may exceed that of *The Man Without a Country*(95).

13. Hale enjoyed harmless hoaxes, such as writing under assumed names or anonymously. At least once the reader was his designed victim: In "Did He Take the Prince to Ride?" *(Atlantic Monthly* [May 1868]), the question, like Frank Stockton's famous "The Lady or the Tiger?" *(Century* [November 1882]), can never be answered.

14. "Hands Off" had special extraliterary significance to Hale as the expression of his theism and paternalism. He regarded it as a basic statement of his religious convictions and published it anonymously (in *Harper's Magazine* [March 1881]) to stimulate a public discussion uninfluenced by his reputation. There was no discussion, but Hale was pleased when a friend wrote him recognizing the authorship.

15. *Our Christmas in a Palace* (1883), pp. 143–44. Hale's readers knew that his "palaces" moved on rails. They were sleeping cars, Pullmans; and, even when snowbound in Iowa and forty-eight hours behind schedule, they were cozy and companionable.

16. Nancy Esther James's discussion of Hale's short stories, which is the core of her dissertation, is fittingly academic and theoretical. With her concern for definition and classification, she has divided and subdivided them more meticulously than Hale did. She calls some "classic" (or matter-of-fact) but more of them "romantic" (extravaganzas); and they are in the form of satires, parables, anecdotes, tales, and historical romances. She analyzes examples of each type, particularly in chapters IV, V, and VII, pp. 54–175, 201–25.

Chapter Five

1. *The Wolf at the Door* has also been attributed to Hale's sister Lucretia. (See Raymond L. Kilgour, *Messrs. Roberts Brothers, Publishers,* [Ann Arbor, Mich., 1952]). Either writer had the social background and the wit which made the story mildly interesting.

2. Except as noted, references to Hale's novels throughout this chapter are to the first editions in book form, as listed in the Selected Bibliography of primary sources: *Ten Times One Is Ten,* enlarged edition of 1883; *Our New Crusade* in *Works,* vol. III; *How They Lived in Hampton,* in *Works,* vol. IX.

3. It is an overwhelmingly sincere tribute to the memory of Hale's friend Frederic Greenleaf, who had died in 1850.

4. From this distance, the adverse review of *Sybil Knox* in the *Nation* does not appear unduly harsh or ill-mannered. Complaining that the book is "too pointedly didactic to win commendation," the reviewer specified further: "In small compass he undertakes to expose the rascality of the

'railroad wreckers', to reprove the disseminators of idle gossip, and to accentuate the moral value of societies formed by women for the suppression of self-recognized faults and the extension of good works" *(Nation,* LV [July 14, 1892], 34).

5. The technical term *Tendenz-roman* is too heavy and pretentious for one of Hale's socially oriented novels, but *adult-Sunday-school-story* is as far astray. As a group, they exhibit a rare combination of generalized appeal for uplift and specific proposals for attainable, practical social changes. Hale recognized his limitations as a novelist. Reading Thomas Hardy's *Far from the Madding Crowd* in 1876, he found it so "wonderfully powerful" that, as he wrote his wife, "such books as this and *Middlemarch* make me ashamed of my novels" *(Life and Letters,* II, 280).

6. Hale enjoyed music, but his casual allusions show no deep appreciation or understanding. Though he was acquainted with numerous performers, his associations were more often with sponsors and supporters of benefit concerts. Such was his participation with Emma Thursby in a midsummer festival at Eliot, Maine, in 1889, which promoted a model cultural center for rural communities. This was a congenial enterprise similar to the efforts described in Hale's novel of the previous year, *Mr. Tangier's Vacations.* Luckily, Miss Thursby, a famous soprano, did the singing; Dr. Hale made the opening day address. (See Richard McCandless Gibson, *The Life of Emma Thursby* [New York, 1940], pp. 362–63.)

7. Hale publicly endorsed Henry Adams's anonymous *Democracy,* Howells' *The Rise of Silas Lapham,* and Bellamy's *Looking Backward.* He also knew Albion W. Tourgée and John Hay, and he could hardly have missed the former's *A Fool's Errand* and *Bricks Without Straw* or the latter's *The Bread-Winners.* Evidence suggests that he had seen H. F. Keenan's reply to Hay, *The Money-Makers* (1885), as virulent an attack upon greedy capitalists as Hay's had been on labor agitators.

8. Hale's denigration of Indians of the seventeenth and eighteenth centuries was conventional. He wrote in Justin Winsor's *Narrative and Critical History of America* (Boston, 1884–1889, 8 vols), I, 325: "The terrors of Philip's War were the origin of the horror and contempt with which for a century men regarded the Indians." Hale disliked them (or thought he did) because of their savagery, not their race; and he maintained that oppression and extermination were never Colonial policy, but rather "the fortunes of war" (in his introduction to N. U. Wallington, *Historic Churches of America* [New York, 1907], p. 22, and in other writings). Although Hale assured the young readers of *A Family Flight Around Home* that "Indians were a grave impediment in the way of the early settlers of New England"(41), he could occasionally be generous in praising their descendants: "Tecumseh and Sitting Bull were men quite as accomplished as the real King Arthur was" *(Boys' Heroes,* p. 76).

9. These names are obviously derived from the didactic tales of Maria

Edgeworth—*Harry and Lucy*(1801), a favorite of the Hale family—and
Thomas Day—*The History of Sanford and Merton* (1783), a favorite of the
Edgeworth family. Hale duly acknowledges his debts to them in his preface
and later; but the story, unlike the theme, is not taken from them.

Chapter Six

1. *Memories of a Hundred Years*, II, 58. See also *Franklin in France* (I,
xiii), where Hale justifies editorial freedom in opposition to the demands of
purists: "We consider it to be our business, in all such affairs, to help and
not to perplex the reader." Hale found no dilemma in the conflicting demands of accuracy and literary grace, praising the possibly "dull" chronicle
(if a choice must be made) of his friend John Gorham Palfrey over the
(alleged) stupidity of Tobias Smollett or the inaccuracy of Scott's *Life of
Napoleon*. (See *Memories of a Hundred Years*, II, 57, 61, and elsewhere.)
He placed more reliance on documents than on either oral tradition or the
press *(ibid.,* I, 138; and II, 68), but he habitually accepted eyewitness
accounts and the private journals and correspondence of participants without enough skepticism or the recognition of processes of exculpation or
rationalization.

2. For example, *Giants of the Republic* (Philadelphia, 1895) with introduction by Hale; also an omnibus one volume *Library of American History,
Literature and Biography*, under doubtful publishing auspices (possibly W.
E. Scull, 1904), for which Hamilton Wright Mabie assumed primary editorial responsibility; *Young Folks Library* (apparently a 1901 set) under the
general editorship of Thomas Bailey Aldrich; *Young Folks Treasury*, in
twelve volumes (New York, 1909), for which Hale was associate editor
under Mabie. I have not seen two titles listed in Mrs. Holloway's bibliography, *Library of Inspiration and Achievement* and *Modern Achievement*,
each in ten volumes, 1903 and 1905, respectively. The overlapping among
such publications is considerable, and the contributions by the "eminent"
writers are frequently only excerpts from their earlier works.

3. Hale's three chapters are on Ferdinand Magellan (II, 591–617), John
Hawkins and Sir Francis Drake (III, 59–84), and "The Naval History of the
American Revolution" (VI, 563–604). In Hale's treatment, they become
chronicles of courageous and socially beneficial exploits. When Hale found a
subject he liked, he used it for as long and in as many ways as he could.
Thus he continued to write and speak on Magellan (*Harper's Magazine*,
LXXXI [August 1890], 357–65) and on Revolutionary naval heroes, as in
Detroit in June 1898 (New York *Times*, July 1, 1898).

4. *General Sir William Howe's Orderly Book at Charleston, Boston and
Halifax, June 17, 1775, to 1776, 26 May*, edited and published by Benjamin
Franklin Stevens, London, 1890, "now first printed from original manu-
scripts" and "with an historical introduction by Edward Everett Hale."

5. As recently as 1965, Claude-Anne Lopez referred to Hale's book in

an elaborate bibliographical note to her *Mon Cher Papa; Franklin and the Ladies of Paris* (New Haven, Conn., 1966) as "old but still useful"(349). In 1975 a writer in *Historische Zeitschrift* (CCXX, 570) cited it in a footnote of scholarly sources.

6. See Whitfield J. Bell, Jr., "Henry Stevens, his Uncle Samuel, and the Franklin Papers," Massachusetts Historical Society *Proceedings*, CXXII (1957–60), 143–211. Although Hale preferred to have the papers deposited in Boston, he publicly urged their purchase by the nation. Says Bell: "Hale's testimony and letter were particularly effective, for they managed subtly to convey both a sense of the value of the papers and the importance of acting quickly"(162).

7. In response to one of Hale's fund-raising appeals, Longfellow wrote "Ballad of the French Fleet, October, 1746" and donated his payment from the *Atlantic* to Hale's project. See vol. III, Standard Library Edition of Longfellow's poems (Boston, 1886–91), pp. 111, 298–301.

8. Space limitations preclude extended discussion of Hale's books for children, a type at which he worked from 1839 (*Jemmy's Journey*) to the end of the century. They were mainly of three kinds: historical and biographical, for general reading suited to adolescents; editions of acknowledged Classics, sometimes abridged but not rewritten; and original fiction crammed with historical and geographical information. As Hale loved children and viewed them unsentimentally as rational young human beings maturing into rational old human beings, the books he prepared for them were not very different from his books for adults. His longer fiction for children, written in collaboration with his sister Susan Hale (beginning in 1881 with *A Family Flight through France, Germany, Norway, and Switzerland*), repeated the faults of his novels but were redeemed here and there by wit and epigram. Nobody from his time, however, could excell his skill in compiling such collections as *Stories of the Sea, Told by Sailors* (1880) or in editing *Arabian Nights: Selections of Stories from Alif Lala wa Laila* (1888) or *Tales from the Travels of Baron Munchausen* (1900).

9. A remark credited to Samuel Bowles of the Springfield *Republican*, as well as to other journalists, ran to the effect that in Boston the only good newspaperman in town (Hale) was being wasted in the pulpit. As Hale often repeated, he rated daily papers inferior to weekly or monthly publications—a prejudice for which the New York *Times* gently chided him (July 9, 1900).

10. As Hale's father had been one of the founders of the *North American Review* in 1815, an opportunity to contribute to the magazine was not difficult to arrange. The current editor was a man Hale greatly admired, John Gorham Palfrey; and the previous editors had all been friends or members of his family, from Jared Sparks through Edward Tyrrell Channing, Edward Everett, and Alexander Hill Everett.

11. *North American Review*, LV (October 1842), 283–302.

12. *Ibid.*, LI, (July, 1840), 213–25.

13. He was also reviewing anonymously for the *Christian Examiner*, certainly by 1848 and possibly from 1844. His assignment was not limited to religious books, for it included history—Bancroft, Parkman, Carlyle—and poetry.

14. *North American Review*, LXXXI (October 1855), 547.

15. *Ibid.*, LXXXII (January 1856), 275–77. Hale's review is discussed in detail in Charles B. Willard's *Whitman's American Fame* (Providence, R.I., 1950), pp. 11–13. In later life, Hale and Whitman seldom met, although they appeared together in public at least once at a meeting of the United States Literary Society, June 26, 1872.

16. Hale's tendency was to consider local government the foundation of public welfare. He believed that newspapers exaggerated the importance of Washington, D.C., "in making up the rigmarole which they call news." See "Social Forces in the United States," *North American Review*, CXXXVII (October 1883), 411, on this subject. In illustration (and incidentally as apology for Republican misconduct), he referred to the still anonymous novel by Henry Adams, *Democracy* (1880), as "a bright and witty satire, very well done," which Hale had discovered was better known in England than at home, "where it had hardly made a ripple in public estimation"(403). To the extent that American "good society" read *Democracy*, "it did not much care that some bright unknown writer who had spent a great deal of life in Europe was soured by what he or she saw in Washington"(411).

17. Quoted by William Sloane Kennedy, "Edward Everett Hale," *Century*, XXIX (January 1885), 338–43.

18. Among the historical essays that Hale reprinted in his collections of short fiction, "The Queen of California" has been the most useful *(His Level Best and Other Stories, 1872).* It is a translation made by Hale that was a genuine contribution to historical knowledge. The etymology of the name *California* had long been in dispute, as it still is. Hale found the name itself, however, in a Spanish romance from 1510, although the earliest edition that he saw was from 1521. Cortez, who discovered the peninsula in 1535, had apparently transferred the name from the romance to the new land; and Hale's article translated the pertinent passages from *Sergas of Esplandian* telling of Calafia, the Amazon queen of California.

19. Hale's association with the *Atlantic*, which started and ended happily, suffered an estrangement of nearly a decade and left a lasting touch of resentment. In a letter to Henry W. Bellows (located in the Massachusetts Historical Society collection), Hale complained in 1878 that the *Atlantic* had ignored him when he started *Old and New*, although it had puffed him ad nauseam while he had been a contributor. As late as 1896, he wrote Charles Eliot Norton (in a letter held by the New York Public Library) to complain that he had never been invited to the legendary *Atlantic* dinners or to the

Saturday Club. James C. Austin includes fourteen letters by Hale in *Fields of the Atlantic Monthly* (San Marino, Calif., 1953), with comments mostly unfavorable to Hale.

20. *Outlook*, LXVI (December 1, 1900) 791–94.

21. *Ibid.*, LXXXVII (November 23, 1907), 625–28.

22. It was designed as successor to the denominational *Christian Examiner* in the hope that it would attract more readers and earn its way. In this respect, it was only partly successful. The account in *Life and Letters* (II, 97–119), from Hale's point of view, is incomplete. See also Earle Coleman, "Edward Everett Hale: Preacher as Publisher," in Bibliographical Society of America *Papers*, 946 (Spring 1952), 139–50; and Frank L. Mott, *History of American Magazines*, (Cambridge, Mass., 1938–57, 4) III, 436–37.

23. A first person narrative, in four short installments of volume two; tall tales of adventures in China, underground, and at the North Pole, with a return to Roxbury via iceberg.

24. *Old and New*, IV (November 1871), 517–26 (by Bellows) and V (April 1872), 474–80 (by Weeden).

25. Most of Hale's verses were also journalism—the response to occasion rather than to a creative impulse. He had some success with patriotic ballads similar to Whittier's, and he wrote other passable poetry without deceiving himself about its merits. His college verses are nicely convivial, and the Phi Beta Kappa poems are appropriate. His most useful verses were those he introduced into his sermons. An old custom with many preachers, it was practiced with particular success by Philip Doddridge in the eighteenth century. As Hale said, Doddridge's sermons are forgotten, but his verses are still sung *(Works*, X, 93). Hale's pulpit verses are far from singable, but they expressed his convictions succinctly.

Chapter Seven

1. On this level of practical ethics, Hale wrote numerous tributes to persons he admired. One significant example is a pamphlet from 1865, *The Public Duty of a Private Citizen*. A tribute to a dead friend, George Livermore, it is also a clear explanation of a type of personality that Hale greatly admired—the public-minded man of affairs, the antithesis of the selfish man postulated, so Hale thought at the time, by Herbert Spencer.

2. Or Sharps rifles, rechristened in recognition of the Reverend Henry Ward Beecher's fund-raising ability.

3. Barbara Miller Solomon, in her *Ancestors and Immigrants: A Changing New England Tradition* (Cambridge, Mass., 1956), makes several complimentary references to Hale's good will, however blurred it was by partial condescension. Her principal discussion occurs in a chapter entitled "The Minority with Faith," pointing out that Hale welcomed immigration for ethical and economic reasons.

4. He also used it for effective lyceum lectures (New York *Times*, May 11, 1889). He favored half-year schools for children (not necessarily for teachers); regretted early dropouts; advocated the abolition of grades and examinations; believed the home should retain moral responsibility; etc.

5. *Nationalist*, I (1889), 37–40. Economic feasibility was common doctrine with Hale. Because of it he was let off easily in a supercilious article by Nicholas P. Gilman in the *Quarterly Journal of Economics* (IV [October 1889], 50–76) as author of "the most practical article which has yet appeared in the *Nationalist* magazine" (65–66).

6. *Cosmopolitan*, X (December 1890), 252–55.

7. *Ibid.*, XI, (September 1891), 632–33.

8. *Ibid.*, XI (April 1891), 121–23.

9. According to a note in the New York *Times* (August 31, 1902), Hale was "the foremost American to advocate the establishment of such a court [as the world tribunal] and has labored to that end for many years." There is little if any exaggeration in such tributes.

Chapter Eight

1. *The Elements of Christian Doctrine, and Its Development.* Five sermons preached before the South Congregational Society, Boston, in January, February, and March, 1860, and printed at its request. (Boston, 1860).

2. Though Unitarians like Hale have been accounted bloodless and unimaginative in comparison to their Transcendentalist contemporaries, they were equally shocking to members of more orthodox denominations. As Harriet Beecher Stowe wrote her son Charles in a letter recently discovered, "I have heard most atrocious radicalism in E. Hale's pulpit," not from him but from "brother ministers" with whom he exchanged guest services. (Quoted by Alice C. Crozier, *The Novels of Harriet Beecher Stowe* [New York, 1969], p. 117.)

3. *North American Review*, CXLII (March 1886), 241. On January 23, 1903, Hale took sacrament in Trinity Church (Episcopal), Boston, at a memorial service for Phillips Brooks. High church members, protesting what they called "sacrilege," attacked their bishop directly and Hale by inference. When Hale was asked who had invited him to participate in the communion, he replied that the invitation had not come from the bishop but that it had been extended "nineteen hundred years ago" (New York *Times*, February 16, 1903).

4. *The Unitarian Principles* (Boston, n. d., but not long after original delivery as a sermon, May 8, 1881), 7.

5. *Ibid.*, 12.

6. *North American Review, loc cit.*, 232, 236.

7. Hale's importance within the Unitarian Church can be followed in numerous specialized publications: George Willis Cooke's *Unitarianism in*

America (Boston, 1902); Charles Howard Hopkins, *The Rise of the Social Gospel in American Protestantism* (New Haven, 1940); Samuel Atkins Eliot, editor, *Heralds of a Liberal Faith*, vol. four, *The Pilots* (Boston, 1952), with a biography of Hale as a leading Unitarian, pp. 150–54, by Paul Revere Frothingham; Henry F. May, *Protestant Churches and Industrial America* (New York, 1963); Conrad Wright, *The Liberal Christians* (Boston, 1970). Hale was so popular among Unitarians that his addresses to church conventions attracted special attention (New York *Times*, September 19 and 24, 1897). After a guest appearance in Oakland, California, in 1891, where he preached the first sermon in a new church, he was amazed at receiving an invitation to a permanent appointment in Berkeley, as he had not suspected that he was under consideration. He declined the call tactfully, unwilling to leave Boston for California. See Arnold Crompton, *Unitarianism on the Pacific Coast; The First Sixty Years* (Boston, 1957).

8. The best information about the printing and sale of these collections is the article by Earle Coleman.

9. Twelve sermons collected into a small book called *Easter* (1886) stress social action. They picture Jesus as the foe of unholy "hucksters," to use Hale's word, and victim of conniving "priests and politicians" of a corrupt "petty provincial capital"(5, 17).

10. Hale followed his principle of conciliation so far that an associate compiled a gilt-edged collection of pious thoughts inoffensive to fundamentalists of any denomination: Mary B. Merrill, *Helpful Words from the Writings of Edward Everett Hale* (Boston, 1893, unp., illus.).

11. " 'Tis Fifty Years Since," in *Sermons of the Winter* (1893), p. 86. J. S. Smith, named as publisher, was Hale's business partner. He directed the *Lend a Hand* periodical and secured republication rights to some of Hale's earlier books. See Earle Coleman's article, and Mrs. Holloway's biography, pp. 224–26. Neither Smith and Company nor *Commonwealth*, a weekly newspaper which that sponsored, was profitable.

12. Brooks, p. 418, note.

Chapter Nine

1. Unless definitely credited, the compliments in this section are typical blurbs used by Hale's publishers. William Charvat, who discussed reviews as scholarly resources in *The Profession of Authorship in America, 1800–1870* (Columbus, Ohio, 1968), unconsciously repeated one of Hale's convictions by saying that "it is a safe estimate that 95 per cent of all past literature, by any definition of that word"(283), has only historical value. Instead of trying to preserve illusions that dead writers remain alive, Charvat declared, "we should be more interested in knowing how far their voices carried in their own generation, and—equally important—whether their generation talked back"(284). Hale's public loved him. All of his books sold well; as Raymond L. Kilgour wrote in his history of Roberts Brothers

(p. 174), "even the most trivial, for Hale was a great figure in Boston life, and his easy, journalistic style seemed to please everyone." The useful compilation by Clayton L. Eichelberger, *A Guide to Critical Reviews of United States Fiction, 1870–1910* (Metuchen, N.J., 1971), pp. 142–44, locates fifty-five notices of Hale's books.

2. The anonymous *Atlantic* reviewer, William Dean Howells, was genuinely enthusiastic over the fresh talent displayed in *If, Yes, and Perhaps*, "the unique and delightful ideality of all the sketches" (XXII [November 1868], 634–35). If he was not so delighted with *The Ingham Papers*, he was still generous in pointing to the "Memoir" of Frederic Ingham as "one of the pleasantest things in the book, which is so full of pleasant things" (XXIV [July 1869], 128). G. L. Lathrop was equally gentle in his *Atlantic* review, eight years later, of *Philip Nolan's Friends*, "Mr. Hale's completest and best novel" (XXXIX [March 1877], 370).

3. *North American Review*, LXXX (January 1855), 114–5 XCII (April 1861), 532–40.

4. *Dial*, XXXIII (1902), 480, 319, 322.

5. *American Historical Review*, IX (October 1903), 184–87.

6. Thanks to the Index, a large number of *Times* reviews can be found without disproportionate trouble. Aside from the "lame and feeble" poems (October 1, 1893) and the pretentious *Franklin in France* (February 27, 1887), the *Times* reviewers approved Hale's work. They described *Our Christmas in a Palace* as "sprightly" (December 10, 1883), *Four and Five* as "capital" (September 20, 1891), and *Susan's Escort* as "inexhaustible entertainment" (August 6, 1897). They praised *Lights of Two Centuries* as "interesting" and informative (November 20, 1887); they favored the *Life of Washington* because it "brings us closer" to the man (January 1, 1888); and, in a long favorable review of James Freeman Clarke's *Autobiography*, they concluded that "Dr. Hale has told the story of this attractive life with sympathy and devotion" (April 19, 1891).

7. *Letters of James Russell Lowell*, edited by Charles Eliot Norton (New York, 1893), I, 333–34. The anonymous reviews immediately following are quoted as printed by Hale's publishers in advertising supplements to his books.

8. Henry A. Beers, *An Outline Sketch of American Literature* (Meadeville, Pa., 1887), p. 204; *Critic*, I, (January 19, 1884) 31, and IV (July–December, 1885), 161.

9. Mildred Howells, *Life in Letters of William Dean Howells* (Garden City, N.Y., 1928), I, 418.

10. "The *Nation!*," Hale exploded to Dr. De Normandie, who was teasing him by mentioning the subject, "I regard it as the most immoral publication in the United States. I wouldn't have it in my home" (James De Normandie, *Proceedings*, Massachusetts Historical Society, XLIII [1900], 11). His wrath should have been appeased by a strangely amiable note on

Susan's Escort (Nation, LXV [October 7, 1897], 282*)* which characterized several stories as "quite triumphantly improbable." Also: "He is one of the last of a band of American writers spiritually attached to the idea of human equality."

11. Dean Charles R. Brown's reflection on the first of these verdicts—which also applies to the second—is that it showed "how much the pew sometimes knows about the pulpit." Dr. Brown was the speaker at the 1922 centenary celebration of Hale's birth, where his topic was Hale as a minister. See his *They Were Giants* (New York, 1934), pp. 115, 125.

12. John Townsend Trowbridge, *My Own Story; With Recollections of Noted Persons* (Boston, 1903), p. 197.

13. Trowbridge made amends to Hale at eighty with references to his "continued marvelous activity" *(My Own Story*, p. 197). "The busiest man" is a description used by Eli Fay (among others), a trustee of Antioch College, as quoted by Austin Craig in W. S. Harwood, *Life and Letters of Austin Craig* (New York, 1908), p. 237. As late as 1918, *Current Opinion*, (LXIV [May 1918], 343) quoted a phrase "lately" applied to Hale: "the most useful man in New England." The pun on Hale's name is credited to "a playful cynic" by Francis Greenwood Peabody, who admitted reluctantly that Hale had tried to do too many kinds of work. See *Reminiscences of Present-Day Saints* (Boston, 1927), pp. 96–97, 111.

14. M. A. DeWolfe Howe, *Barrett Wendell and His Letters* (Boston, 1924), p. 91,

15. Bliss Perry, *And Gladly Teach* (Boston, 1935), pp. 230–31. Hale's best friends recognized this weakness. Dr. De Normandie, noting that Hale read "everything" with lightning speed, admitted that he also "remembered a great many things which he never read . . . and what he did not remember he easily imagined" (9–10).

16. George F. Hoar, *Autobiography of Seventy Years* (New York, 1903), II, 441–42.

17. *Outlook*, LXXXVI (June 22, 1907), 425. In an introduction to "Colonel Clipsham's Calendar," Mabie's praise covers several facets of Hale's work: "no one has better understood the secret of democracy"; his writing has "wonderful freshness of feeling" as well as "inventiveness, humor, and Defoe's faculty of treating imaginary and even improbable situations as if he were making a record of fact"(425–26).

18. Mrs. Bernard Whitman, *Cosmopolitan*, VI (March 1889), 439.

19. *Harvard Graduates' Magazine*, XI (September 1902), 91.

20. *Letters of Theodore Roosevelt* (Cambridge, Mass, 1951), III, 248.

21. *Ibid.*, VI, 1200, 1289, 1334.

22. Ida Husted Harper, *Life and Work of Susan B. Anthony* (Indianapolis, 1908), III, 1599.

23. *Review of Reviews*, XXIII (May, 1901), 549–57.

24. Helen M. Winslow, *Literary Boston of Today* (Boston, 1902), pp.

36–37. The author, with more enthusiasm than discrimination, praised every Boston writer whom she knew; and she was widely acquainted.

25. Hoar, *op. cit.*, II, 445.

26. *Ibid.*, 448.

27. *Ibid.*, *loc. cit.* The Phi Beta Kappa representative, Professor Edwin A. Grosvenor of Amherst, reported that "the spirit of the occasion transcended words" (Oscar M. Voorhees, *History of Phi Beta Kappa* [New York, 1945], p. 302). Numerous references to Hale throughout the book show his unflagging interest in the society.

28. *Review of Reviews*, XL (July 1909), 79. Compare "the New Englander who became neighbor to the whole country," as Hamilton Wright Mabie wrote in his formal obituary for the American Academy of Arts and Letters, reprinted in *Commemorative Tributes of the American Academy of Arts and Letters* (New York, 1942), p. 21.

29. *Nation*, LXXXIII (June 17, 1909), 604–05.

30. Clara Barrus, *Life and Letters of John Burroughs* (Boston, 1925), II, 193.

31. Lilian Whiting, *The Golden Road* (Boston, 1918), pp. 46–47.

32. Lyman Abbott, *Silhouettes of My Contemporaries* (Garden City, N.Y., 1921), p. 160; Henry James, *Charles W. Eliot* (Boston, 1930), II, 309. Other references to Hale's mottoes occur on I, 14 and II, 301. A comment by Eliot's brother Samuel, Hale's close friend, applies to a period about 1870: "More and more his motto was that of Dr. Hale which he often quoted and thoroughly illustrated"(I, 317).

33. Francis G. Peabody, *Reminiscences of Present-Day Saints* (Boston, 1927), p. 95.

34. M. A. DeWolfe Howe, *The Atlantic Monthly and Its Makers* (Boston, 1919), pp. 46, 103.

35. Ernest E. Leisy, *The American Historical Novel* (Norman, Okla., 1950), p. 119; Arthur Hobson Quinn, *American Fiction* (New York, 1936), p. 207.

36. Fred Lewis Pattee, *Development of the American Short Story* (New York, 1923), pp. 183–85.

37. Gamaliel Bradford, *Journal of Gamaliel Bradford 1883–1932* and *Letters of Gamaliel Bradford 1918–1931*, both edited by Van Wyck Brooks (Boston, 1933 and 1934), p. 202 of the *Journal*; and *Letters*, pp. 29–30, 98, 101–102.

38. William James, *Varieties of Religious Experience* (New York, 1902), p. 82. Compare Edwin D. Starbuck, *The Psychology of Religion* (London, 1900), pp. 305–307, who found Hale's outgoing optimism highly productive of good. George S. Merriam, who knew Hale much better than William James did, stated emphatically that "in truth, he had his full share of heart-wringing sorrow" *(Outlook*, XCVI [November 12, 1910], 587.

39. Bradford, *Letters*, p. 101; *Journal*, p. 202.

40. George M. Fredrickson, *The Inner Civil War; Northern Intellectuals and the Crisis of the Union* (New York, 1965), pp. 117–18.

41. New York *Times,* January 7, 1899.

42. *Dial,* XLI (December 1, 1906), 390.

43. Reissue of several of Hale's books by offset process in small editions indicates a survival of scholarly attention rather than a general revival: three volumes in the American Short Stories Series (New York, 1969): *James Russell Lowell and His Friends* (1965), *Sybaris and Other Homes,* and *How They Lived in Hampton* (1971). *Kanzas and Nebraska* was made available on microfilm (Ann Arbor, Mich., 1956), and an expensive, handsomely printed and illustrated edition of *The Brick Moon* was distributed by the Imprint Society of Barre, Massachusetts, in 1971. Hale's apt phrasing has recently been utilized by a writer in the *Journal of Negro History* (LX [1975], 109, footnote 67); and it is a talent of Hale that merits further exploitation.

44. Paul S. Boyer, "Boston Book Censorship in the Twenties," *American Quarterly,* XV (Spring 1963), 3–24. In the Watch and Ward Society, Hale was in the company of an almost complete "directory of Boston's reformers"(5), New England college presidents, and the Boston *Transcript*(7).

45. Robert Taft, *Photography and the American Scene* (New York, 1908), p. 20.

46. S. H. Woodbridge, *Overthrow of the Louisiana Lottery* (1921), as cited in Stokes and Pfeffer, *Church and State in the United States* (1964 ed.), p. 305; Robert A. Woods and Albert J. Kennedy, *The Settlement Horizon: A National Estimate* (New York, 1922), pp. 37, 51, 126. Also, Nathan I. Huggins, *Protestants Against Poverty* (Westport, Conn., 1971) a study of Boston charities between 1870 and 1900; this book shows the significance of Hale's contribution to reform: "the absence of crisis in the thinking of Hale is what distinguishes him most sharply from his liberal predecessors"(42).

47. Stanley T. Williams, *The Spanish Background of American Literature* (New Haven, Conn., 1955), I, 74, etc.; Samuel Eliot Morison, *The European Discovery of America: The Northern Voyages* (New York, 1971), pp. 104 and 110 note, citing Hale's references to Brazil in the *Proceedings* of the American Antiquarian Society, 1873; J. T. Trowbridge, pp. 197–98, on roses; and W. S. Kennedy's *Century* magazine article (January 1885) on "Yankee Doodle." Arthur Mann deserves commendation for his thoughtful references to Hale's significance in *Yankee Reformers in an Urban Age* (Cambridge, Mass., 1954), pp. 11–17, 77, and 252, n. 31.

Selected Bibliography

PRIMARY SOURCES

"A Checklist of the Writings of Edward Everett Hale" by Jean Holloway is virtually complete and accurate. It was published in three installments of the *Bulletin of Bibliography*, XXI (May–August, September–December, January–April, 1954–55), 89–92, 114–20, 140–43) and was divided into the following sections: books and pamphlets, 144 entries; sermons and addresses, 101 entries; books edited, 23 entries; contributions to books by others, 86 entries; contributions to periodicals, 510 entries; short pieces in collections with no known prior publication, 28 entries; a partial listing of separate editions of *The Man Without a Country* in English, 34 entries.

The titles listed below include Hale's principal books as quoted or mentioned in the text. Significant complementary shorter writings are cited in the section of "notes and references."

Books by Edward Everett Hale

Back to Back; A Story of To-day. New York: Harper and Brothers, 1878.
Boys' Heroes. Boston: D. Lothrop and Company, 1885.
Christmas Eve and Christmas Day: Ten Christmas Stories. Boston: Roberts Brothers, 1873.
Christmas in Narragansett. New York: Funk and Wagnalls, 1884.
[Clarke]. *Autobiography, Diary and Correspondence of James Freeman Clarke* [edited, with extensive contributions, by Hale]. Boston: Houghton, Mifflin and Company, 1891.
Crusoe in New York, and Other Tales. Boston: Roberts Brothers, 1880.
East and West; A Story of New-born Ohio. New York: Cassell Publishing Company, 1892. (Also called *The New Ohio, a story of East and West.*)
Elements of Christian Doctrine and Its Development. Boston: Walker, Wise and Company, 1860.
Every-Day Sermons. Boston: J. Stilman Smith and Company, 1892.
A Family Flight through France, Germany, Norway, and Switzerland. Boston: D. Lothrop and Company, 1881. [In collaboration with Susan

Hale; followed by *A Family Flight Over Egypt and Syria*, 1882; *A
Family Flight Around Home*, 1884; *A Family Flight through Mexico*,
1886; by the same writers and publisher.]

The Fortunes of Rachel. New York: Funk and Wagnalls, 1884.

The Foundations of the Republic. New York: J. Pott and Company, 1906.

Four and Five; A Story of a Lend-a-Hand Club. Boston: Roberts Brothers,
1891.

Franklin in France. 2 vols. Boston: Roberts Brothers, 1887–88. [In collaboration with E. E. Hale, Jr.]

From Thanksgiving to Fast. Boston: George H. Ellis, 1879. [Fifteen sermons, paged separately.]

G. T. T.; or, the Wonderful Adventures of a Pullman. Boston: Roberts
Brothers, 1877.

The Good Time Coming; or Our New Crusade. Boston: Roberts Brothers,
1875. (Later titled *Our New Crusade; A Temperance Story*.)

His Level Best and Other Stories. Boston: Roberts Brothers, 1877.

Historic Boston and Its Neighborhood. New York: D. Appleton and Company, 1898.

History of the United States. New York: Chautauqua Press, 1887.

*How They Lived in Hampton: A Study of Practical Christianity Applied in
the Manufacture of Woollens*. Boston: J. S. Smith and Company, 1888.

How To Do It. Boston: J. R. Osgood and Company, 1871.

If Jesus Came to Boston. Boston: Lamson, Wolffe and Company, 1895.

If, Yes, and Perhaps. (Four possibilities and six exaggerations, with some
bits of fact.) Boston: Ticknor and Fields, 1868. (Later titled *The Man
Without a Country and Other Tales*.)

The Ingham Papers. Boston: Fields, Osgood and Company, 1869.

In His Name [first edition, Boston, *Old and New*, 1873]. Boston: Roberts
Brothers, 1888.

James Russell Lowell and His Friends. Boston: Houghton, Mifflin and
Company, 1899.

June to May; The Sermons of a Year. Boston: Roberts Brothers, 1881.

Kanzas and Nebraska. Boston: Phillips, Sampson and Company, 1854.

The Kingdom of God, and Twenty Other Sermons. Boston: Roberts
Brothers, 1880. [Paged separately]

Letters on Irish Emigration. Boston: Phillips, Sampson and Company, 1852.

The Life in Common, and Twenty Other Sermons. Boston: Roberts
Brothers, 1880. [Paged separately]

The Life of Christopher Columbus. Chicago: G. L. Howe and Company,
1891. (Another title: *The Story of Columbus as He Told it Himself*,
1893.)

The Life of George Washington, Studied Anew. New York: G. P. Putnam's
Sons, 1888.

Margaret Percival in America: A Tale. Boston: Phillips, Sampson and Company, 1850. [In collaboration with Lucretia P. Hale.]

Memories of a Hundred Years. 2 vols. New York: Macmillan Company, 1902. Revised edition, with three added chapters, 1904.

Mohonk Addresses. Boston: Ginn and Company (for the International School of Peace), 1910. [By Hale and David J. Brewer.]

Mr. Tangier's Vacations, a Novel. Boston: Roberts Brothers, 1888.

Mrs. Merriam's Scholars. Boston: Roberts Brothers, 1878.

My Friend the Boss; A Story of To-day. Boston: J. S. Smith and Company, 1888.

A New England Boyhood. New York: Cassell Publishing Company, 1893.

The New Harry and Lucy: A Story of Boston in the Summer of 1891. Boston: Roberts Brothers, 1892. [In collaboration with Lucretia P. Hale.]

Ninety Days' Worth of Europe. Boston: Walker, Wise, and Company, 1861.

Our Christmas in a Palace, a Traveller's Story. New York: Funk and Wagnalls, 1883.

Philip Nolan's Friends; A Story of the Change of Western Empire. New York: Scribner, Armstrong and Company, 1876.

Prayers in the Senate. Boston: Little, Brown, and Company, 1904.

The Rosary of Illustrations of the Bible. Boston: Phillips and Sampson, 1849.

Sermons of the Winter. Boston: J. Stilman Smith and Company, 1893.

Seven Spanish Cities, and the Way to Them. Boston: Roberts Brothers, 1883.

Stories of War Told by Soldiers. Boston: Robert Brothers, 1879. [Followed by *Stories of the Sea Told by Sailors*, 1880; *Stories of Adventure*, 1881; *Stories of Discovery*, 1882; *Stories of Invention, Told by Inventors and Their Friends*, 1885; all published by Roberts Brothers.]

The Story of Massachusetts. Boston: D. Lothrop Company, 1891.

The Story of Spain. New York: G. P. Putnam's Sons, 1887. [In collaboration with Susan Hale; alternate title: *Spain.*]

Studies in American Colonial Life. Meadville, Penn.: Flood and Vincent, Chautauqua Century Press, 1895.

Susan's Escort, and Others. New York: Harper and Brothers, 1897.

Sybaris and Other Homes. Boston: Fields, Osgood, and Company, 1869.

Sybil Knox; or, Home Again; A Story of To-day. New York: Cassell Publishing Company, 1892.

Tarry At Home Travels. New York: The Macmillan Company, 1906.

Ten Times One Is Ten: The Possible Reformation. Boston: Roberts Brothers, 1871. [Later editions with slight revisions 1883, 1893, 1899.]

Ups and Downs; An Every-day Novel. Boston: Roberts Brothers, 1873.

"We, the People"; A Series of Papers on Topics of To-day. New York: Dodd, Mead and Company, 1903.

What Career? Boston: Roberts Brothers, 1878.

The Wolf at the Door. Boston: Roberts Brothers, 1877. [Anonymous]

The Works of Edward Everett Hale. "Library Edition." Ten volumes. Boston: Little, Brown, and Company, 1898–1900.

SECONDARY SOURCES

Few scholarly research articles and only two books have been written about Edward Everett Hale. Both books are highly competent biographies with well-founded literary commentary: *The Life and Letters of Edward Everett Hale*, in two volumes, edited by E. E. Hale, Jr. (Boston: Little, Brown, and Company, 1917), and *Edward Everett Hale: A Biography*, by Jean Holloway (Austin, Texas: University of Texas Press, 1956). Nancy Esther James's doctoral dissertation, as described below, is meritorious.

Short articles specifically about Hale are more often friendly tributes to his personal qualities than rigorous analyses of his writings. The following are useful for information and interpretation. Significant incidental data about him in works on other subjects have been identified in the Notes and References.

ABBOTT, LYMAN. "Edward Everett Hale, an American Abou Ben Adhem." In *Silhouettes of My Contemporaries*, pp. 100–25. Garden City, N.Y.: Doubleday, Page and Company, 1921. Recollections of a friend of many years; written late in life.

COLEMAN, EARLE. "Edward Everett Hale: Preacher as Publisher." In Bibliographical Society of America, *Papers*, 946 (Spring 1952), 139–50. Centers on three of Hale's ventures: *Old and New*, printed sermons, and partnership with J. S. Smith.

DE NORMANDIE, JAMES. An untitled formal tribute to Hale in *Proceedings*, Massachusetts Historical Society, XLIII (1910), 4–16. Anecdotes by a disciple who shared Hale's wit as well as his convictions.

HIGGINSON, THOMAS WENTWORTH. *Carlyle's Laugh, and Other Surprises*. Boston: Houghton Mifflin Company, 1909. Obituary reminiscences of Hale (pp. 159–72) by a contemporary and lifelong friend; reprinted from the *Outlook*, XCII (June 19, 1909), 403–406.

HOWE, M. A. DeWOLFE. "Edward Everett Hale." In *Dictionary of American Biography*, VIII, 99–100. New York: Charles Scribner's Sons, 1932.

JAMES, NANCY ESTHER. "Realism in Romance: A Critical Study of the Short Stories of Edward Everett Hale." *Dissertation Abstracts International*. XXXI (1970), 1802A. Abstract of an unpublished dissertation, Pennsylvania State University, 1969. The dissertation itself is an informative, thorough investigation (367 typewritten pages) of Hale's shorter narratives, with evaluations of their technical adequacy, readability, and relation to the development of realism.

KENNEDY, WILLIAM SLOANE. "Edward Everett Hale." *Century*, XXIX (January 1885), 338–43. Biographical and critical; factually accurate and discriminating.

Index

141